Fearless

To Christos and Myles—my favourite people in the world.
Thankyou for giving me the best chapters of my life.

Contents

CHAPTER ONE

A Family Who Loved to Celebrate (1966–1982)

I COME FROM A large Italian family, and I remember my childhood as a time of festivities and family celebrations. I am third in line of the pecking order, with two older sisters and a younger brother.

My mother was one of eight siblings, as was my father. He came to Australia with his family in 1950 and my mother's family arrived in 1954. Like many migrants, they had an amazing work ethic and a spirit of optimism, which they instilled in their children. I grew up with a sense that life, with all its opportunities, was going to be fabulous.

I had twenty aunties and uncles so there was always a party going on; there seemed to be cousins everywhere we looked. Family and friends, but mainly family, were always around. Many of our relatives were called Frank, Joe and Billy. My brother, Ben, even inherited the name Billy for a while. Despite feeling lost in the crowd at times, I had a sense of belonging and of being loved. There was always a lot of noise, loud voices, loud TV, music and laughter. Amongst the ordered confusion there was plenty of food and an expectation that we would all contribute to the conversation. There were definitely no rules that children should be seen and not heard. We all competed to tell the best joke. Jerry Lewis was our favourite actor.

In between parties, we would sit for hours on a Sunday afternoon watching movies: *The Three Stooges*, *The Nutty Professor* and, of course, *Epic Theatre*, *Variety Italian Style* and the wrestling. I still recall the name Mario Milano, which is interesting given I tend to forget people's names. My mother would be in the kitchen cooking pasta and schnitzel, the smell of delicious food wafting through the house. Life was good.

Mum came to Australia with her mother and siblings when she was nine. She made the journey by sea after her father had been here for two years, working to save enough money for the rest of the family to come over. My grandmother was forty-six when she arrived in Australia. I can appreciate now how much courage that journey must have taken.

My maternal grandparents had five girls and three boys. Sadly, two of the boys passed away in Italy, one from diphtheria at twelve months of age and the other of peritonitis at age twelve. Their third son died in Australia at age nineteen from rheumatic fever. I don't think my grandmother ever recovered.

She was a character, that's for sure, a bit mischievous and always on the go. She would walk for miles every day to buy groceries for the family. She separated from my grandfather in the early 1970s as she wasn't willing to stay in a marriage that clung to olden-day rules and that hadn't evolved since she left Italy in the 1950s. She lived until she was ninety-four and always remained a strong matriarch in our family.

My father came to Australia with his family when he was fifteen, also by sea. He told me about his visions of grandeur when he arrived. He knew Australia was the lucky country, compared to the devastation of post-war Italy where everyone was starving. His parents arrived here broke but ambitious and open-minded, with a plan to give their children greater opportunities in life. I never met my father's parents; they passed away before I was born.

My father's courage paid off. He re-invented himself many times over the years; he worked hard and was success-ful. Necessity, after all, is the mother of invention. He raised us with a work ethic that only develops within someone who has been in need, and he instilled in us values of humility, love and celebration.

My parents met through my paternal aunty; she and Mum were school friends. At age thirteen, Mum was betrothed to Dad, so their marriage was only a matter of time. They married when Mum was sixteen and my father twenty-seven. The arranged marriage was typical of many Europeans of the time; it was not questioned, just simply arranged, as it had been for generations in Italy.

By the time my mother was twenty-one she had four children. Her life was hectic, to say the least. My brother, Ben, was the youngest of the four siblings, with Bettina the eldest and Teresa in the middle. We were all very close growing up; also very close in age, five years between us all. My mother tells stories of us all getting sick together. She would quarantine the house for weeks on end, with one of us giving a bug to the other, and then the chain of contagious ailments would start again. At times she found herself throwing up in tandem with the rest of us.

We grew up on a large property in Brighton, a bayside suburb of Melbourne. The home had once been an orchard, so our backyard was huge and lined with fruit trees, vegetables and roses. It was set on a train line but, strangely, I can't remember the sound of the train going by. The noise was probably drowned out by the rowdy chaos inside the house. There was enough room for all the cousins to play, a vegetable plot and chickens in the back coop. We had fresh eggs every morning and chickens for Sunday lunch, which my grandmother would cook. Having loved animals from a young age, I was disturbed that my grandmother could transform the life of a chicken into a Sunday roast, and I couldn't eat chicken for many years. Moreover, the smell of a freshly plucked chicken boiling in the kitchen was not very appealing—though no-one else seemed to mind.

One day the chickens escaped from their cage. The four of us went into the backyard as usual, but this time we were met by angry chickens that chased us around. It had never happened before and we were terrified. As we climbed to safety on the swings and up in the trees, I realised we'd been ambushed and now we had to work out how to get back inside. Mum came out flapping a tea-towel, shooing the chickens away, commanding us to 'Run!'. I was impressed by her fearlessness. 'Mum, why are the chickens chasing us?' I remember asking, but never worked it out. I was told some theory about them being fed meat, which had made them eat their own eggs and therefore become aggressive.

The next day the chickens were gone, replaced a week later by two rabbits. Perhaps my parents weren't aware of the saying 'breeding like rabbits'; needless to say, within months there were so many rabbits in our backyard that we couldn't count them. There were rabbit droppings everywhere. Rabbits everywhere. I can't recall how or when we got rid of them, but I'm sure our rabbits contributed to the rabbit population of Melbourne.

We had moved into that property when I was three years old. I vaguely recall the day we moved in. I was in trouble for drawing stick-figure pictures on the wall with texta and for enthusiastically jumping on the couch with my brother and sisters. It was a game we all loved, and my mother had to replace our couches frequently; the 1970s spring system just didn't seem to hold up. I still have images of large silver springs poking out of 1970s upholstered fabric.

Our weekends were endless fun. We would go for long drives with the family, which usually meant a convoy of cars, each boot crammed with enough food to feed a village. We'd arrive at our destination, either the beach or the country, the car boot would open and fill the air with the aroma of gourmet food. It didn't matter whether you were hungry; no-one could refuse an offer of schnitzel, pasta, lasagna, stuffed peppers, stuffed eggplant, roast chickens, salads and, of course, all the desserts: cannelloni, watermelon … the list goes on.

It was all about food; we often set out on an adventure to go cherry- or strawberry-picking, or we'd end up in the country where the men could shoot quail. I much preferred picking berries as the sight of dead birds distressed me.

Christmas was always the most fun; I especially loved Christmas morning. The routine was the same year after year. My sisters and I shared a bedroom, and my father, who had a super-8 camera, would film us getting up, walking from our bedroom to my brother's bedroom and then running to the Christmas tree, tearing paper and excitedly piling up our presents. The night before, we'd leave milk and cookies and a note for Santa. As the years rolled on, at my father's suggestion, we'd leave out beer instead of milk, thinking Santa would enjoy a drink. This was my first experience on camera. Looking back, I can only say that no-one will ever see my hair that messy on film again.

My favourite Christmas gift was a large doll in a pink dress, which strangely had ash-blond hair that looked suspiciously green and smelt like nylon. So I called her Nylon. Quite insightful for a five-year-old to know about nylon; but, after all, the 1970s were all about nylon and plastic. So my next favourite gift was a large yellow plastic kangaroo and the reward for decapitation was a belly full of chocolates. The smell of plastic-infused chocolate is still with me.

The relatives would arrive in the morning. The party would begin with platters of food and the exchange of gifts; there'd be music, more noise and cousins everywhere.

I always had a sense that anyone who visited who wasn't family was somehow orphaned and had no relatives to celebrate with.

Easter was also a lot of fun. There was a stronger religious focus at Easter than at Christmas which tended to be distracted by gifts and food. Easter was the only time of year that I was aware I was Catholic. We'd go to midnight mass and were given gifts of religious significance, such as a cross or a medallion with the head of Jesus wearing a crown of thorns. The movies we watched were also strong reminders of the meaning of Easter, such as *Ben Hur*, *The Ten Commandments* and *Jesus of Nazareth*, all courtesy of *Epic Theatre*.

I loved having a young mother and large family, but the demands of young children so close in age took its toll on my mother who became exhausted. I'd hear my father tell her, 'Anita, snap out of it.' At the time, I didn't understand what he meant. Was he was trying to get her to stay calm amongst the chaos? He wanted her to be able to cope, but she simply ran out of steam. The strain of four pregnancies from age sixteen had compromised her health. As a young mother she hadn't had the opportunity to finish growing.

Boarding school was the remedy. 'Let the nuns look after the children for a while,' I heard my father say. 'After all, Prince Charles goes to boarding school.' I was six years old at the time and found this very confronting.

My time at boarding school is a bit of a blur, but several episodes stand out. It felt like a lifetime, but I was only there for six months in 1973 while my mother had a well-earned rest. Being pulled away from a life of celebration and abundance to live with nuns who prided themselves on martyrdom, scarcity and discipline was certainly a challenge. Being in the country, several hours away from home and family, made it all the more unbearable.

We arrived at Sacred Heart Convent in winter, mid-year, at what felt like the middle of the night because I had fallen asleep in the car on the way there. It was probably only around six o'clock in the evening but it was dark and cold, a typical Ballarat winter's day. As we pulled up I looked over to Bettina and Teresa who were embarking on the same journey. The boot was full of luggage and we were already dressed in our new school uniforms, which included a woollen beret. Staring ahead, I saw a school that was set behind a huge eight-foot red-brick cloistered wall adjacent to a red-brick convent of enormous proportions. I can't recall if Mum was with us, I just remember my father trying to coerce me out of the car and then pinching me on the arm to get me through the front gate. Needless to say, I didn't want to be there at all. I had come from the local primary school where Mum would pick us up every day in a fabulous car, wearing a fabulous outfit. But life was about to change.

I started to cry. I knew I had to pull myself together as I didn't want to be teased by the other girls. There was no way out of this; my father was leaving without us. So I walked through what felt like prison gates into the convent: my first bite at courage. I couldn't indulge my fear or protest any more. I had to deal with the situation. For the first time I had to 'snap out of it'. Suddenly the words my father had said to my mother made sense.

The front door led into a large old entrance hall with heritage tiles and a heavy wooden staircase. It was freezing cold. I clung on to my beret. The students had just finished dinner and were in the kitchen washing their dishes. I met some of the older girls who I never recall seeing again. They distracted me for long enough to allow my father to slip away unnoticed—but only temporarily. I started to run towards the front door to find him, but the girls pulled me back. This was it. Sink or swim. I remember that I stopped talking, as though I was in shock that he had actually gone through with it. He had left.

My sisters and I were taken upstairs to our dormitory. Thank God we were all in the same dorm; I was terrified that we'd be separated. The room was large with lots of windows and housed boarders from Prep to Grade Six. I was in Grade Two, Teresa in Grade Three and Bettina in Grade Five. Bettina was nine years old, Teresa was eight and I had

Dear Mom,

This may come a bit early (hopefully it won't come late!) but I just wanted to wish you a Happy Mother's Day!!

I've told Gina about you and how you have been fighting a lot to get through hard times this year!

She stresses that you need to keep on smiling!

-Roxy

just turned seven. There was a large statue of Our Lady next to a small cubicle where our dormitory nun slept. We were required to sit at the foot of the statue and practise saying 'Hail Mary' prayers every night as part of our rosary. This was my first significant encounter with religion.

Every morning Sister Damian would walk into our dorm, chanting the 'Our Father' prayer in her loud voice. She was our alarm clock. We were expected to get out of bed immediately and go to our allocated basin to wash for breakfast. Showering was done the night before. Lights went out at around eight o'clock and no-one was allowed to make a sound. The only light you could see was the lamp in the nun's cubicle as she unveiled. I was fascinated by the image of her shadow as she removed her veil. She was a rotund lady with long black hair. I learned very quickly that she shouldn't have been caring for children as she delighted in meting out physical punishment and spiritual fear.

One night one of the students, who suffered epileptic seizures, was talking in her sleep. Suddenly all the lights went on and as punishment we were made to strip our beds, pull the mattresses onto the floor, remake the beds on the floor and kneel beside it reciting the 'Hail Mary' prayer fifty times. Then we had to strip our beds again, put the mattress back on the base, remake the bed and go to sleep. Most of us didn't know what was going on. We had been asleep so hadn't heard the talking. I mistakenly thought it was morning so I put on my teddy-bear slippers with the googly eyes and little pink tongue, and as I pulled on my pink quilted dressing gown, the rotund dormitory nun strapped me for not standing to attention. Bettina looked on in horror. Not at all harsh, don't you agree?

I became friends with the only other girl in Grade Two. She was from New Guinea and was boarding with her older sister and cousin. I had never met anyone from New Guinea but had heard there were witch doctors, cannibals and headhunters there. She reassured me that neither she nor her family was any of the above. Apart from one other girl in Prep, we were the youngest boarders at the school.

There were many day-scholars in Grade Two, but not enough to fill a class so we shared our classroom with Prep and Grade One students. Unfortunately my class teacher was the same nun from our dormitory. For the sake of not identifying her, I'll call her Sister Psycho. Her abusive approach was relentless. She'd find any excuse to strap me in the evening and humiliate me during the day.

One day at school, my friend was hugging me and saying, 'Gina is my best friend.' As Sister Psycho walked in, she started yelling, 'Lesbians! You are lesbians!' My God, what did that mean? Such a big word that I'd never heard. She aggressively pulled us apart and told us that as punishment we had to stand in the corner and kiss the wall until recess. We stood there rocking backwards and forwards for two hours kissing the wall, confused about what a lesbian was and why kissing the wall was the remedy.

My experience at boarding school was an endless series of horror stories. I felt terrorised. I learned about hauntings, how students and nuns had died and where their spirits loitered. A small toolshed behind the school was where a nun had allegedly been hammered to death. Staying in the shed for fifteen minutes with her unrested soul was part of an initiation into a group of Grade Five students. On the wall of the piano room hung a framed picture of a young girl; apparently she had died at the piano in that room. We were told that if we misbehaved, Satan would come and take us from the stairs leading up to our dormitory. We were told that a student who had been knitting in the sickbay had reached over and pierced her lung with a knitting needle and died. We heard that the ghost of a nun who had died in the convent was often seen walking around with black thread on her lips that had been stitched closed when she died. My God, where was I?

I decided that I would never go anywhere alone and stuck by my sisters like glue. We were often heard whispering to each other in the middle of the night to come to the bathroom. We had to be extremely quiet. We didn't want to strip beds again.

The staircase leading up to the dormitory was always scary. Despite our fear, we would often play there. One day Teresa and I were enthusiastically sliding down the banister, as children do. Teresa stood at the top of the stairs and said, 'Watch this.' I watched her jump from the top step onto the old shiny wooden balustrade. With her belly sliding along, slipping freely, she said, 'No hands!' As she picked up momentum, her legs flew up in the air and she slipped straight over the top of the handrail head first onto the mosaic floor below. Her head hit the concrete with a mighty thud. In a panic, I ran to the top step and screamed at the top of my voice. Then I ran down the stairs to find her lying on the floor, her head bleeding. There was dirt everywhere from a pot plant that had fallen off its stand. Fortunately, the plant had broken Teresa's fall. She jumped up and started running and screaming. I chased her. No-one came to our aid. The students nearby thought we were just having an argument so they didn't react until they saw the blood.

Teresa was taken to the hospital that night. I was so happy to see Mum and Dad and wanted them to take me home. I hated that staircase even more than ever. I hated the school. I felt like I was in an orphanage with children who had been rejected or abandoned by their parents. Teresa came back that night. She was okay. A case of concussion with a small cut on her forehead.

We were desperate to leave. We were not having a good time at all. Teresa and I would sit for hours clapping hands together and making up songs. We would sing:

I had a boarders' fever, I had it really bad.

They wrapped me up in blankets and put me in a van.

The van was very shaky, it almost shook me out,

And when I got to the boarding school, I heard a boarder shout,

'Oh Mummy, Daddy take me home from this awful boarding school,

I've been here a year or two and I just want to be with you.'

Here comes Sister Angela, sliding down the banister.

Even though she's mad with me I asked her for a cup of tea.

The college, which was established in 1881 by the Sisters of Mercy, felt haunted with dark corners and shadows cast by dim lighting. It was always freezing cold, inside and out. There was a distinct smell of old carpet and wooden floorboards created an orchestra of creaks and echoes. The building was described as one of the most clandestine buildings in Ballarat; it was a labyrinth of rooms and staircases with a rich history. These days it's an abandoned place of worship and forms part of a local 'Ghost Tour'. I hear the locals pride themselves on its haunted history.

The fear I felt in that school compelled me to pray. I would often go to chapel with the nuns before breakfast. We were required to wear a mantilla—a piece of lace cloth— to cover our hair. Mine was black; some of the girls had white lace.

Teresa and I made our Communion that year. I auditioned to sing solo and got the gig. My parents came to school with Ben and I sang my heart out in the haunted chapel.

Mum and Dad visited most weekends. Sometimes my cousins would come along and we'd go out for Sunday lunch. It was a welcome relief from the bland convent food. The nuns were very strict about our diet. We were allowed Vegemite on toast only once a week. The older students would hide jars of Vegemite under the tables in the dining room and the younger students were rewarded with a pat on the back for finding the hidden jars. The nuns loved pies. Shepherd's pie, fish pie, mashed-up mystery-bag pie. Teresa hated pastry and would dry-retch at times. But apparently vomiting was not a good enough excuse to forgo your dinner. We were punished for not eating, and Teresa was forced to carry a plastic container with her for a week—Sister Psycho thought that the humiliation would be a good lesson for spoilt behaviour. I wonder if she ever saw the movie *Oliver Twist*?

Watching my sisters being abused by the nuns was really tough, almost harder than managing my own abuse. Teresa had exchanged letters with another boarder. They would make fun of the nuns and each letter was signed off with 'X' for kisses, as girls do. The letters were found by Sister Psycho. With her spirit of perversion, she counted up the number of kisses combined in the letters and strapped the girls with a leather belt, delivering one strap for each X (kiss). There were forty-eight kisses. Now I was getting angry. I think we were all getting angry. Bettina was more proactive in her responses. She pelted a tin of Cool Mints at the head of a student who made me cry, calling out 'Merry Christmas Christine!' as the tin struck the girl's forehead. I wanted to run away, but for the first time we were becoming very protective of each other. I couldn't leave my sisters behind. In the past we had argued, pulled each other's hair, fought like girls, like sisters. Now we were a team. We had arrived as children and were going home as girls. Little did we know this would not be the last time we'd have to look out for one another.

Christmas came and we went home for the school holidays. We were told that we were not going back to Ballarat; Mum had had her rest. No doubt she saw how traumatised we were. Apart from coming to terms with being away from family, we had to digest the deranged, abusive and perverted thinking of Sister Psycho. We had lost our innocence and unfortunately had been shown a terrible side of Catholic education that was marked by relentless abuse. This experience impacted on my religious views and on my innocent faith that had been nurtured through *Epic Theatre*. My mother spent many years trying to repair the damage. She would talk about God all the time and read the bible to us. She gave me a bible when I was twelve. I was so curious about faith that I read it from cover to cover and realised that Sister Psycho was simply evil and had nothing to do with God. She was a fraud, posing as a nun in a convent. She never once taught us about the doctrine of Christianity: love and forgiveness.

Happy to have that chapter of my life behind me, I decided to never look back. I loved being home. I was so relieved to be with my family again that I appreciated everything.

*

IN 1974 WE started a new school: Sacré Coeur in Glen Iris, Melbourne. The school was founded by the French order of nuns, the Society of the Sacred Heart. I was relieved to learn that it had nothing to do with the order of nuns in Ballarat. It was a happy and positive school, so for a change I was happy and positive. Once again, Mum would pick us up each afternoon. My parents had a Chrysler dealership so Mum would drive a different car from the car yard most days. She would turn up in a range of convertibles and sports cars, dressed like she had just stepped out of Italian *Vogue*:

high heels, hairpieces, sometimes turbans, even a blonde Afro. She always looked fantastic and the world seemed to stop when she arrived. She often wore plush colours like chocolate-browns and navy blues with suede boots, coloured hosiery and nail polish to match.

Business was booming. At twenty-nine, my mum was driving a Rolls Royce and all her children were in private schools. She loved shopping and every Friday night she would take us into the city. We would come home with bags of clothes and excitedly spill them out onto the bed.

As well as being beautiful, my mum was very strong and forward-thinking. She raised us to believe that the world was ours for the taking and we should go out, work hard and get what we wanted without fear. She was a visionary who taught us that we had only ourselves to rely on, that no-one would come to our rescue, that if we wanted something we had to go out and get it. 'In life you need faith, wisdom and success,' she'd tell us. These were her guiding principles.

Success was very important. It could only be achieved through hard work and determination. We weren't allowed to indulge in being emotional, tired or weak. Even when we were sick she would get us out of bed. She didn't want us to become fragile or frail. She wanted to see strength and resilience at all times. She admired people who were street-smart and down to earth, and she had no time for snobs, show-ponies or flirts. She strove to raise sensible, intelligent, composed children who would one day become high-achieving adults who looked and felt good. We weren't permitted to wear jeans, sneakers or tracksuits. We wore 'liberty' dresses and imported shoes. Mum's influence no doubt formed the foundation of our love for fashion and our drive to succeed.

Practising what they preached, my parents worked hard in their car business, which they'd named Tina Motors after Bettina. Everyone knew Nick and Anita: the Italian man with the young beautiful wife. Influenced by his Italian heritage, my father also wore suits tailored from the best imported fabrics, custom-made by his own full-time tailor. In all honesty, he probably needed a tailor given he was only five-foot-seven with a belly that one can only develop from a good life and Australia at that time wasn't known for its fashion. In fact, it was four seasons behind European fashion—which I discovered from flicking through Italian *Vogue* and European fashion magazines that my mother imported to the local newsagent.

As a result of Tina Motors' booming success, in 1975 we moved from our big property to a house on the beach in Brighton. It was a stately two-storey home with bay views all around. For the first time, we each had our own bedroom. My mother furnished our house with gilt mirrors, antique furniture, crystal and Venetian glass chandeliers and plush fabrics from Italy and France. Anything she could find that was gold-leaf embellished she would buy. Huge gold mirrors hung in our bedrooms. We had gold bedheads quilted with silk damask and matching bedspreads and curtains in pale blue and pale pink. Our home felt a bit like the Palace of Versailles, with Louis XVI furniture everywhere; it was opulence at its best.

My mother's bathroom was furnished with white carpet and stained-glass windows. She would sit on a large French gold-upholstered footstool in front of a gilt mirror to apply her makeup and blow-wave her hair. She wore beautiful sleepwear: I remember a flowing cobalt-blue crushed velvet silk robe with matching heeled slippers and baby pink negligees with matching robe and slippers. Her nails were always perfectly manicured. I would sit and watch in awe of her beauty. She smelled divine.

I loved living on the beach and spent the whole summer in a bikini, swimming and sunbaking. We made a lot of friends in our street; there were children in every house. At the end of the street was a laneway that lead to the beach. Ours was the corner house opposite the laneway. It was the perfect stretch of footpath for skateboarding and riding bikes. With ABBA, the *Grease* soundtrack and the Bee Gees' *Saturday night Fever* playing in the background, we were torn between disco and dagsville. We learned to disco dance and would practise renditions of 'Mamma Mia', Teresa being Freda while I was Agnetha.

One year, we were thrilled to have an opportunity to wait backstage at an ABBA concert. But I mean really far back—like behind the chicken-wire fencing at the back of the concert hall where the band climbed into their limos to be whisked off. I recall a huge crowd behind us waiting for a glimpse of the band. I was there with Teresa, my aunty and two cousins. We were so excited to be in the front row at the back of the stage at the back of the carpark at the back of the chicken wire. As the band members emerged, the crowd pushed forward and I watched as Teresa's face was pushed into the chicken wire as she tried to avoid triangular dissection. We all left with chicken-wire indentations from head to toe. It was risky business being an ABBA fan, but we loved it. We collected every ABBA fan card we could find and accumulated enough bubblegum to last us a lifetime.

*

WE MOVED SCHOOLS again in 1976 when I was in Grade Five. This time we attended St Michael's Grammar School a few suburbs away from home. It was my first co-ed experience. I was at school with my sisters and my brother. My two younger cousins, with whom we were very close, also attended the school. They lived with my grandmother, my aunty and their younger brother. My grandfather had passed away earlier that year and my aunty had separated from her husband while we were at boarding school. Her husband was a dishonest man, with a gambling problem, who had done jail time for embezzling money from my parents' business. The two girls were like my little sisters. I was very protective of them, as we had all become of each other over the years. We spent a lot of time together at school and after school at my grandmother's house.

My grandmother didn't speak English, despite being in Australia since 1954. We learned a very old-fashioned way of speaking Italian with her, a blend of dialect and broken English. In fact, we made up our own language, inventing words such as 'supermarketa' for supermarket, 'milky-barro' for milkbar, 'ticketa' for ticket, 'la keka' for the cake, 'undundies' for underwear. She seemed to understand us just as we understood her.

My grandmother was an amazing woman, entirely self-less. She was up early every morning cooking for the family. She never drove a car so walked everywhere and caught public transport. She wore black every day in perpetual mourning for her sons who'd died. She was never counselled and never spoke about losing her boys. She took her loss in her stride, like so many women of her generation who had lost children. The only thing she ever taught me about her loss was that you should never question how someone copes with grief and loss. She believed that if you asked the question, the universe would come to test you. She remained Italian to her core, steeped in the traditions of the village where she grew up. She practised Italian home remedies, followed her superstitions and cooked copious amounts of food every day. She was the ultimate Italian grandmother. She never missed out on anything to do with her grandchildren or great-grandchildren. It was clear to me that you can take a woman out of a country but you can't take the country out of a woman.

Teresa and I were probably the closest growing up and spent a lot of time together. We were the middle children so we never got the attention of the eldest or youngest child. Being one year, one month, one week, and one day apart, we were also the closest in age. In 1976 we were in a composite Grade Five–Grade Six class. Teresa was much more disorganised at school than I was. I kept all my pencils in a pencil case, which was named, all my books were covered in contact plastic and I strived to be the model student. Teresa was arty and creative and didn't think about being organised. We would start the school year with the same stationery but within weeks, she'd be borrowing my things because hers were lost or she'd left them at home.

We had the same sense of humour and would laugh for hours about anything—the way Mum pronounced a word, a piece of fluff on someone's nose. It wasn't even the fluff that was funny; it was noticing the same thing and seeing each other's reaction. We were especially amused when we got into trouble. At times we would react as though we were being tickled, laughing so hard that there was no noise, only a clicking at the back of our throats—which would make us laugh even harder. Whenever I was in trouble with Mum, Teresa would stand behind her while I was being told off and pull faces. She'd push up the tip of her nose and poke out her tongue. The more I laughed the angrier Mum got. We often used humour as a way of coping with stress. We were so close that despite having our own bedrooms I always slept in Teresa's bed. She understood that I was still traumatised by our boarding school experience, plus my bedroom was at the top of the stairs which made me the first port of call for an intruder, or if Satan came to visit.

Bettina was a couple of years ahead of me at school so to me she always felt like one of the 'big' girls. I would invariably go to her if I needed help or if I was worried about something. She was more reserved than Teresa and very focused on her friends at school. I was the annoying little sister who would tell Mum everything. As an older schoolgirl, she was in a different wing of the school so I didn't see her often, but when I did I was always so excited. She and her friends fascinated me; they were just becoming interested in boys and were dressing up and painting their nails. Every Friday night they would go to the local disco at the YMCA. Bettina would wear either hot-pink or black disco pants and high heels. Her cutting-edge fashion was inspired by Olivia Newton-John in *Grease*. I couldn't wait to join her. Turning twelve seemed to be taking forever.

One day Bettina was in an art class next door to my classroom. I saw her through the glass door and started waving enthusiastically. Her friend said, 'I think your sister is waving at you.' Bettina, as cool as she was, gave me a reluctant wave. I went skipping off, thrilled that I had seen her. As I approached the heavy door at the end of the corridor, one of the students let it go just as I was walking through. When the glass door swung back, I raised my hand to stop it, but my arm went through the glass, resulting in a deep cut below my elbow. I called out to Bettina, 'I've cut my arm, I've cut my arm!'

Bettina later told me that she heard, 'They've cut my heart, they've cut my heart!' She didn't come to my aid as she was paralysed with fear so I ran to her and she looked away, expecting the worst. Relieved that I was holding my elbow rather than my heart, she rushed me down to sickbay and waited until my aunty arrived to take me to the doctor.

I ended up having ten stitches and a respite from school for a few days to recover.

Ben was in Grade Three, in the little school. I would go looking for him in the playground at recess and lunchtime and always found him in the sandpit. He was a sweet little boy who kept us frequently amused with stories he'd been telling since he was in kinder. How Miss MacDougal had drunk ten bottles of milk 'but she didn't die'. I had a warm affection for him as a big sister. We had an interesting connection, often dreaming the same thing or saying the same thing at the same time. He loved tomato sauce sandwiches and bananas and we would sit together after school watching *Gilligan's Island*, *Bewitched* and *I Dream of Jeanie*. We spent hours playing with Lego and had been known to play in the mud as children, then run through the white sheets hanging on the clothesline. I think we swung on a few clotheslines and broke them along the way. He was quieter than my sisters. He probably couldn't get a word in so sat back and observed a lot.

*

IN 1977 WE moved schools again, this time to Firbank, a local girls' grammar school which was walking distance from home. This was my fifth school and I was only in Grade Six. I really hoped this was it. I could feel myself becoming more socially awkward. Was this due to my age? Entering adolescence is never easy. I felt the girls to be very cold in their approach. Was it the grammar influence? Maybe I preferred a Catholic influence, minus the nuns. There was one girl in particular who thought calling me a 'wog' was okay. The taunting started in Grade Six and continued into Year Seven. I didn't care about the word; I was more upset by her level of contempt for me for no reason other than my nationality. I had never been called a 'wog' before, nor had I ever been teased. I might have been looking more like a wog as I was growing out of my baby face.

One day I'd had enough of her. We were standing in the bathroom at the washbasin and she started the taunting. I turned around, picked her up, put her in the plastic rubbish bin and rolled her down the stairs. I never said a word. I went back to the classroom, retrieved my schoolbag and walked out of the school to the sound of girls cheering in the background. Evidently, she hadn't only picked on me. I had been pushed too far and I'd lost my cool.

It was my first experience with a bully. I knew that if such a thing were to ever happen again, I would have to bend a bit longer before I broke. I wasn't proud of my reaction. I didn't like that this girl, who was irrelevant, had affected me to the point of making me snap. I promised myself that I would never again let an idiot get the better of me.

When I got home I told my mother what had happened. Like a good Italian mother, she thought the girl deserved it. She probably did deserve a serve of my wrath, but nevertheless, I was embarrassed. I had become a bully like she was and there was nothing about her that I wanted to emulate. Then and there, I decided that I would never let anyone dictate my standard of behaviour. I was going to be me, and if someone didn't like it, it was his or her problem.

At school the following day, suddenly I was very popular. I was a tough girl who had earned a lot of respect, and no-one ever picked on me again. I didn't have to say much, the girls just knew what I was capable of. I became the go-to girl if anyone was being bullied. All I had to do was walk into a situation and it was immediately diffused. I was completely intolerant of bullying and would make bullies apologise for their behaviour. Although I was only in Year Seven, my calling in life was already beckoning. Despite my plan to study medicine, I was destined to defend the underdog.

Things were not great at home. My parents had been arguing a lot and were having financial difficulties. They say that when money goes out the door, love flies out the window. The recession of the 1970s was affecting businesses across Australia and we were feeling it too.

We spent more and more time at my grandmother's, sometimes staying there overnight and on weekends. It was an escape from the arguments. Despite living in the beautiful surroundings of our home, life was becoming less beautiful.

After fifteen years of marriage, my parents decided to separate. I was thirteen years old. It felt like the world was caving in.

*

DAD MOVED OUT for the first time in January 1978, taking only a small colour television with him. From memory, my parents were still working together in their Chrysler dealership. A staff member alerted my mother to a woman who was spending a lot of time with my father. My father had wanted to employ her, and this became the subject of a lot of their arguments. We knew what was going on, nothing was done behind closed doors in our family. My mother found out where this woman lived and went with my aunty to visit her. They knocked at the door but no-one was home. Peering through a gap in the front window, they got a glimpse of the front room and noticed the colour television; Dad had been caught out. Anxiously, they waited in the bushes for someone to come home. Sure enough, there Dad was, driving up the street and parking in front of the western suburbs flat. Mum jumped out of the bushes and ran towards him. In a panic, he took off.

Ignorant of the goings-on at her home, the woman turned up with her young daughter. Mum confronted her about my father, and it was on. The woman attacked my mother and my aunty had to come to her aid. They arrived home with scratches and cuts and with a big story to tell my grandmother who had been babysitting us during the fiasco. They didn't appear to be at all concerned that we could hear everything that had happened. We all sat and listened to the story as it was told, with a sense of bravado that 'we got him, the truth is out'. There was no shielding us from the perils of life. Our mother wanted us to be aware of the ways of the world.

My father denied having an affair. My mother didn't believe him but, like a lot of women who discover their partner's infidelity, she weighed up the loss of the family unit and the impact of separation on her children. My mother had worked so hard to give us a beautiful life; she wasn't going to let another woman interfere with that.

Although she did not protect us from the world and people's behaviour, my mother was very vigilant about our safety. We were not allowed to go out the front gate on our own, sleep at friends' houses, and school camps were only reluctantly permitted later in school life. She wanted us to be streetwise and, as a good Italian mother, thought fear and the occasional dose of guilt were an effective deterrent. My father was the protector; she wasn't going to relinquish that in a hurry.

I adored my father but became confused about my parents' marriage. My father's betrayal had warned me to never trust men. My mother had grown up in the 1950s and was raised to believe that a woman is defined by her husband. According to this mindset, a woman is nothing without a man; she's a spinster—in other words, a failure. But my mother was simultaneously influenced by the 1960s generation of free love and women's rights, so she was not prepared to put up with anything that impinged on those rights. How could she ever be happy? She was nothing without a man but she could never trust the very thing that defined her.

I pondered this dilemma for a long time, wondering how I could reconcile this apparent contradiction and eventually find the man of my dreams. Ultimately, I decided it was easier to never allow a man to define me. This meant I should not be financially dependent. I would have to run my own race. It was a defining moment for me. I started to think about how I would achieve this independence. Eventually I realised that the solution was to pursue a career that would make me financially self-sufficient. I became very focused on my schoolwork, believing this to be my ticket to happiness and success.

My parents reconciled for a short time. Mum was trying to negotiate with the finance company to trade out of debt.

They took out a second mortgage on the house to finance the business. Despite their efforts, Chrysler had suffered a global loss from the oil crisis in the late 1970s and, as America plunged into recession, the car industry fell into depression. My parents couldn't get stock to sell from overseas and had to close down Tina Motors.

Eventually Dad moved out again. I learned that it is very difficult to recover from resentment. Dad went to live in Perth; his cousins were there and worked in the car trade. He went chasing a buck and to start again. I missed him terribly and would speak to him regularly on the phone after school. In his Italian accent, he would tell us that he missed and loved us, saying, 'I love a-you.' Then he'd complain about the hot weather. It was the first time he ever wore thongs—not the underwear, but the type you wear on your feet.

After Dad moved out we changed schools again. This time it was mid-year and we turned up in the uniform of our former school as without much notice of our crisis, we hadn't had time to get new uniforms. It was an interesting experience going to co-ed Brighton High School wearing a private school girls' uniform; the taunting started quickly and I was called all sorts of names. 'Hey, did you catch the wrong bus to school?' This was school number seven and I was in Year Eight. Fortunately, our old uniforms were quickly replaced, although not forgotten.

On the positive side, my two older cousins were at the school, Pat and Robert, both of them avid Collingwood football supporters and very popular boys. They were hilarious guys with big personalities whom everyone loved—the class jokers, but no-one's fool. Pat was the older brother. His large stature commanded respect and his sense of humour was infectious; he was the Jerry Lewis of the family. As a young boy, he'd gather all the cousins and get us to follow him around the backyard chanting, 'The king of the world is Pasquale'—and we believed him. He was a born salesman and a lifesaver at our new school. Word got out that we were his cousins and life was sweet.

As in every school, there were different categories of students. There was a clique of cool kids, a group of daggy students, and loners who would get teased because they had acne or ate bananas for lunch. I often found myself defending anyone who was the victim of teasing. I deliberately befriended the students who were shunned and I did it with the bravado and security of knowing my cousins were there to protect me. No-one challenged me.

At this stage of my life I had started to develop resilience. It became survival of the fittest. Dad was gone and so was our beautiful life. Mum valiantly tried to hold things together, but our regular family gatherings started to fall away and we seemed be growing apart from our relatives. My mother and her younger sister grew closer and we spent a lot of time with her and her children. She was a strong woman with a loud voice who loved to sing Elvis songs, tell inappropriate jokes and go to discos. She taught us how to disco dance and we would all get together, including Mum, and dance for hours to blaring music. We would watch Molly Meldrum's *Countdown* on the ABC every Sunday night and music and dancing became our escape.

Mum starting selling women's clothing from home, assembling most of the designer labels that she could find in Australia. Brighton women flocked to our home to buy and soon the front room, filled with baroque antiques, was turned into a clothing store. Mum hosted fashion parades and did photo shoots for newspapers with models wearing some of her creations made from coloured silk scarves with gold thread. She eventually moved her wares into a retail store in the local street, naming the shop Anitella which means 'little Anita'. With her great eye for fashion, her store was very successful. We were quickly trained as salesgirls. Mum was excellent at delegating. We had grown up with her list of chores, from washing and ironing, to doing the dishes, sweeping the floors, dusting, cleaning mirrors, cooking and being at her beck and call for anything she couldn't reach. We were expected to step up to the mark at all times. If we didn't do it properly, she would stand over us, pointing, until we got it right.

Eventually we had to sell the family home. Dad wasn't having much success in Perth and the mortgage, which was security on the business, had been called in soon after the business closed. Every time the house was open for inspection we would clean frantically in an effort to achieve the best possible price. My aunty and her three children would come over to help.

One day the agent arrived a bit early for an open for inspection. When the front doorbell rang, we all ran out the back door, my aunty still holding the vacuum cleaner. We hadn't worked out where we were going and it was raining, so we all piled into her car in the driveway—seven children, one adult and a vacuum cleaner. The car started to steam up, which concealed us from the passers-by who were coming to inspect. In fact, my aunty, who was always a bit mad, told us to breathe heavily onto the glass to create more fog so we couldn't be seen. I still laugh at the memory of us squashed into a car, potential buyers seeing us breathing heavily at the windows.

The house was purchased by one of our neighbours. His wife and Mum were best friends and Teresa and I had become best friends with their two daughters. They had an older brother who was extremely good-looking; he was a surfer with long blond hair and drove a kombi van. Through him we discovered the world of surfie culture. He would take his sisters, Teresa and I down the coast to watch him and his friends surf. He listened to Pink Floyd, Tubular Bells and a lot of music from Virgin records.

We started to invest in our own music collection. We'd go to the local record shop and buy vinyl albums. We were trying to be cool, collecting any album that was charting well. We also tried to buy albums that were less known and part of the surf culture. Unfortunately, we couldn't always remember the names of the bands so we'd go home with a Deep Purple album instead of Pink Floyd. We knew it was a colour; we just couldn't remember which one!

We also got our first look at German pornography. Although it was soft pornography, like *Playboy* magazine, I was amused that one of the younger girls became fascinated by a photo of a naked man when she discovered that a man's testicles are not anatomically placed above his penis.

Our neighbours were a German family who had done exceptionally well in their export business of meat supplies and abattoirs. The father drove a gold Mercedes Benz and the wife drove a matching one in silver. They had a grand backyard with a swimming pool and built-in trampoline. Beside the pool was their pool house/cabana where they would often throw parties and light up the garden with open-flame totem poles. We learned all about German cuisine, apple strudel and goulash. They had three Corgis and a

Rottweiler named Prince, all fed eye-fillet and morbidly overweight. The Corgis would sleep on the kitchen chairs and snore loudly.

Later that year we moved into another house in Brighton, around the corner from my grandmother's house. It was a large old two-storey home with the internal staircase boarded up and crammed with furniture from our larger home. Other people lived upstairs. The house had not been renovated since it was built in the 1940s. Strangely, a cupboard in one of the rooms still contained old photos belonging to past residents. That room still seemed to house those residents, and there was always a cold swell of air in there. We refused to sleep in that room; instead, the four of us slept in one room and Mum slept in the front sun-drenched bedroom. It was a terrible, spooky house with lots of noises, but we drowned out the creepy ambience by playing music and watching television. We would dance all weekend and after school.

Our public high school education was short-lived. Mum couldn't cope with the change in our disposition, our language, our smoking, our focus on boys and the fact that the schoolteachers were not at all interested in anything she had to say. So, almost predictably, we started at another school, the local Catholic girls' school. The nuns at Star of the Sea College were from the order of Presentation nuns so I was hoping they'd be different to the nuns at boarding school. I was still in Year Eight, and at a new school wearing my former uniform. Dear Lord, when was this going to end?

Sure enough, the taunting began again, 'Did you catch the wrong bus to school…?' By this stage I was so over it, I just ignored the girls and stayed focused on going to class. It was very different from my last school experience where I had said 'sorry' that many times on my first day that the girl sitting next to me eventually told me to stop apologising.

As I sat in my Year Eight class, for the first time in a long time I felt calm and at peace. My class teacher, Miss Godfrey, had a gentle approach and didn't push the students around. She gave us the time we needed to complete the work at hand. I felt very stable and comfortable in her class and I hoped that I was there to stay. I started excelling in my studies, putting in a tremendous effort to please her. I was so thrilled to be given an A+ for a Christmas project that I have kept the assignment to this day.

A few months after we sold our home, our German neighbour who'd bought it offered it back to us for rental. We were thrilled and moved back in. Unfortunately, the move was short-lived as our neighbour became embroiled in a meat scandal that ultimately closed his business and saw him flee to Germany to avoid a jail sentence. He had been selling kangaroo meat, passing it off as beef. Sadly, he took off with his wife's best friend and his children never saw him again. I wasn't surprised that he'd run off like that; he had often made advances at my mother who was a loyal friend to his wife.

Mum sold off most of her beautiful Louis XVI furniture to keep afloat. Our next home was a two-storey house around the corner with a swimming pool. We were okay with the move but we loved our old house and I was very sad to leave. I loved living there and vowed to work hard when I grew up so that I could move back there one day.

Mum was still selling clothing but had relocated the business back home. One weekend she decided that we would get up at four o'clock in the morning to set up a stall at a country market to try to sell off the balance of her stock. Reluctantly, we agreed to go with her. She always made us feel like we had a choice, even though we knew that saying no was not an option.

We arrived at our destination and unpacked the car. As we waited for some customers to turn up, I decided to take a look around this market full of bric-a-brac. In my travels I came across a pet store. There were kittens, puppies and rabbits in cages. I walked straight past the rabbits—wasn't going there again—and over to the puppies. Wiggly fur bodies jumped and yapped excitedly at anyone who passed by; and then I saw her: a little golden Beagle cross Cocker

Spaniel puppy asleep at the bottom of the pile, a white diamond marking on her forehead. She was covered in dog piddle and the faeces of her sibling pups; I fell instantly in love and wanted to rescue her from the bottom of the pile. I picked her up and hugged her. Gently, she licked my chin and then yawned, her puppy breath in my face. She was sixty dollars and I was determined to keep her.

I ran back to my mother at the stall and excitedly told her about the gorgeous puppy. Dragging Mum to the pet store, I lifted the puppy out of the cage and hugged her to show the mutual love. I think Mum realised that she wouldn't manage to prise the puppy away from me so she paid for her and I walked out of the pet stall with my new best friend. All the money Mum had made that day went towards the purchase.

Teresa and Ben were thrilled. They loved her. Bettina was a bit indifferent, never a dog lover. We went home broke with another mouth to feed but deeply satisfied that we'd rescued a puppy in need. On the way home we decided to call her Honey, given her colour and that she was so sweet, a little honey.

*

IN 1980 OUR financial situation became more difficult. When our lease was up we had to move again. Our new home was close by—an old, olive-green, federation-style home with ugly chocolate-brown carpet and linoleum kitchen floors. It only had three bedrooms so Teresa and I had to share. The house was nestled behind a chemist on the corner of a main road opposite the beach. It had a wooden return verandah at the front with a high wooden fence and front gate. We loved that it was across the road from the beach, so the location made up for the ugliness. All our friends lived close by. We were growing up and our friends started driving cars.

I wanted to help Mum financially, so that Christmas, when I was fourteen, I started in a job during the school holidays at the local dog-wash salon. The dogs were so cute when they were wet. They loved a good scrub, and having their ears tickled always made them shake off the excess water, which regularly showered me in the spray. The tough dogs were the cutest. Despite being aggressive towards other staff members, they always seemed to be obedient with me. I would make strong eye contact and they'd immediately retreat.

I wanted Christmas morning to be fun so I spent every cent I earned on Christmas presents for my family. We put up the Christmas tree that was still decorated with ornaments from our childhood. Mum was touched by my effort. By Christmas morning I had managed to fill the area under the tree with gifts. We spent Christmas Day at my grandmother's, celebrating with all my cousins. We were still adjusting to Dad being gone. It's amazing how the absence of one person can have such an impact. The world felt different without him.

We spent that summer on the beach with Honey, the same beach we'd played on when we were living with Dad. I felt at home there and loved that we were living near our old house.

Bettina was in her last year at school and Teresa was contemplating leaving school while I remained focused on achieving high enough grades to study medicine. Mum was working hard to look after us. Dad hadn't helped her out financially for a long time. He had come back from Perth and set up another car yard with his brother. He had a new partner and it looked like marriage was on the cards. He'd moved in with the woman and her daughter and he was making a fresh start.

After my parents separated they never spoke again. Despite the distance between my parents, I remained very fond of my father and always looked forward to seeing him. He was fun to be around, always loving and affectionate. Every Sunday he'd pick us up and take us to lunch at the local pizza parlour. To me it seemed that his lack of help for Mum was because he was trying to get back on his feet. He had suffered the same loss after the marriage breakdown as my mother, although he didn't have four children living with him that he had to clothe and feed.

I remember visiting him at his apartment when he lived alone. He seemed sad and lost. He once told me that some weekends he would go home from work and not talk to anyone until he went back to work on Monday. I felt disturbed that he was lonely and would often call him during the week and on weekends to say hi. I was relieved when he eventually found a partner; I never wanted him to be lonely again.

Mum had taught us that no-one is going to rescue you; you can only rely on yourself. In her determined way, she found an empty shop-front around the corner from home and opened another clothing store. It was both disappointing and inspiring to see my mother practise what she preached. Disappointing in that she was in such a difficult position; yet inspiring in that she took control of her situation. It was a hippie-type store across the road from the beach. We took it in turns working there after school and on weekends. Mum still had a good eye for fashion and the shop was successful. We had sold clothes before, so we knew what to do.

I was now in Year Ten; I had managed to stay at Star of the Sea. It was the first time in my school education that I had been at a school for longer than a year. Mum—who seemed to have got lost in all the stress of getting divorced, adjusting to being a single mother, moving house and moving schools— was finding herself again. She was only in her early thirties and had developed a strong social network. She went out frequently and hosted dinner parties with friends. We were still friends with our German neighbours so would go with them to the German club for lunch. One weekend we had photos taken by the in-house photographer who presented them to us in cardboard frames. We took the photos home and placed them on the mantelpiece in the living room.

Mum had also started socialising with my cousin Mara who was studying law. She had moved out of home with her boyfriend who was also studying law. One afternoon they came over to our house with a friend. Mum wasn't home so Ben let them in and they waited for Mum to get back. While they were waiting, they noticed the photos on the mantelpiece. The uni friend pointed at the photo of Mum and enquired who it was. 'That's my mum,' said Ben. The friend challenged Ben saying, 'No, that's not your mum, she looks too young.'

I don't know when my mother met the uni friend or how that meeting went; all I know is that she married him the following year and is still married to him. Needless to say, her decision to marry him created some chaos. He wasn't about to move in with four teenage children so in order to plan a life together she decided to close the shop and move out of our home. I was in Year Eleven and very suddenly had to make some serious decisions about what to do next.

CHAPTER TWO

Determined to be Educated (1982–1985)

I N 1982 I was fifteen years old and in Year Eleven at Star of the Sea College. Teresa had left school that year to pursue a career in fashion. Bettina had finished school and was working with my father at the car yard. She had moved out temporarily to live with some friends; Mum's delegatory ways had caused them to clash at times. I missed Bettina not being at home but it seemed quieter with her gone. Teresa and I had separate bedrooms for a while, our cousin Rosie was also living with us and slept in Teresa's room; she was fourteen and attended the same school. Ben was also fourteen, and still at school.

I was studying hard, determined to pursue a career in medicine and had chosen my subjects accordingly. I was achieving good grades and it looked like I was on my way. I had set up the tiny back room as a study and worked on my assignments and homework every night for three hours after school and for six hours each Saturday and Sunday. I saw my education as my ticket to independence and success. I had been a mischievous child in the past couple of years at school, but I knew I had to knuckle down if I wanted to achieve my goal. By mid-year I was topping my class. My teachers encouraged me to work harder. I had become friends with my class teacher and my art teacher. I loved art history. It was the only subject I was studying out of love, not necessity. Most of the other teachers were just teachers, and there were only a few nuns at the school, including the head mistress. They were a dying breed. I didn't know anyone who wanted to become a nun and, from my childhood experience, I understood that they weren't much fun to be around.

We weren't aware of it at the time, but during this period Mum was dating her husband-to-be. She was spending less time at home and more time with him. We didn't mind the freedom her absence gave us. Teresa was going out a lot and Bettina, who had moved back home by now, was rarely around. I spent many mornings getting myself ready for school and making my own way home.

Dad remarried in October 1982. My mother seemed startled by this news. She had assumed the burden of parenting us without his help. She wanted him to share some responsibility and not behave like a lot of fathers do post-separation: their only connection to their children being to count them: 'Oh yes, I have four children …'

It was a tough journey for Mum and she made constant sacrifices to ensure we were okay. After my father remarried, she decided that it was time for her to marry her new partner and move out of our home. She rang my father for the first time in years, to tell him her plan and to get his promise that he would look after us—he agreed. Dad would have to pick up the pieces. Ben was fourteen, I was sixteen, Teresa was seventeen and Bettina was eighteen.

Ben went to live with Dad and his new wife. I was just finishing Year Eleven, sitting my final exams, and didn't know what to do now that Mum was moving out. I had come home from school one Thursday night to find her leaving with a removal truck, taking her bed and most of the furniture. I had known she was going but wasn't really prepared for it. She took most of her furniture, thinking I would go and live with my father.

It was a bit of a Mexican stand-off when I saw her. Both of us had things to say but avoided saying much at all. I tried to help her by getting empty boxes from the milkbar around the corner. I remember walking down the street, frowning, a heavy burden over me. I really didn't want her to go.

I should have asked her not to, but it was too late: she was on her way out the door. She had left with a promise from my father that he would look after us and she was expecting that her absence would lead me to my father's house. I knew I didn't want to go there, and change schools again, but I didn't tell her.

As the front door closed behind her, I ran to my neighbour's place, hoping to find my best friend at home. I let myself in through their back door, walked into the living room where he was watching television and sat on the couch next to him. I didn't speak. I just sat. He looked at me and asked what was wrong; I obviously looked distressed. I told him that Mum was gone.

'What?' he asked, not following what had happened.

I explained that my mum had moved out. The removal truck had taken most of the furniture and she had just left. I started to cry.

He reached over and hugged me, and with the sweet bravado of a fifteen-year-old boy, he said, 'I promise that you will be alright, I will look after you.' He really meant it.

I knew that, in reality, he couldn't do anything to help me. But the fact that he cared was enough. He was one of six children of an Irish family, the youngest of the three boys. They had come to Australia from Belfast a few years before and were in a similar situation, their mother also raising them alone. We had met when he was twelve and became childhood sweethearts. We thought we'd get married one day but I always seemed to have a boyfriend who got in the way. In fact, my current boyfriend—a tall, good-looking blond boy who loved to surf—wasn't happy about my friendship with my Irish sweetheart so he banished me from seeing him. But this didn't stop me from going to his house the day Mum left. We were still best friends, I knew I could trust him and that he would understand my dilemma—unlike my boyfriend, who I broke up with soon after Mum left.

I went home later that evening once I had recovered from Mum's departure. There was a messy void in the house that I was determined to fix straight away. I moved beds and rearranged the house with the furniture that was left. I was up all night cleaning and vacuuming. How could such a positive time in her life feel like such a terrible time in mine?

The next day I went to school and sat my final exams. I didn't tell my teachers about my dilemma until the end of the following week, on my last day of school. They had noticed that I wasn't my usual self; I was looking tired and particularly serious. I was generally a high-energy girl who laughed a lot, especially when I was stressed. But now I wasn't just stressed, I was angry.

I was angry that I was faced with the problem of where I was going to live when all I wanted to do was finish school and become a doctor. If I stayed with my sisters I knew that my chances of a high academic achievement were diminished without Mum at home; I would be competing against students who had a mum to bring them cups of tea and nurture them into university.

I confided in my favourite art teacher. Despite my anger, I was somewhat embarrassed about my predicament, and worried that she'd form a negative opinion of my mother. After all, I hadn't told Mum that I didn't want her to go, and I did think she deserved an opportunity to live her life and be happy. But I was now becoming aware of how this was impacting on me.

My art teacher took me to see the headmistress. At first, I didn't see the purpose of this visit, but as soon as I was seated in front of Sister Josepha, it became clear that I had a lot to say. I expressed my anxiety about my future and the choices I faced. I explained that I wanted to finish school and achieve high marks so that I could study medicine. I told her that my father lived far away and that if I went to live with him I'd have to change schools, which I didn't want to do. Also, I didn't want to be separated from my sisters. I said that I didn't know how I'd manage living on my own: I couldn't pay for school fees or buy my books for Year Twelve. I didn't want to ask my parents. My father had not been supporting me financially to date and I didn't want to burden my mother with these expenses; nor did I want her to tell me to go and live with my father.

For an hour, Sister Josepha listened to me spill my grievances. In my anger and grief, I blurted that I should just throw it all in. I felt that my mother leaving had pushed me into a corner with nowhere to go. In anger I suggested that I become a street kid or a drug addict or anything degenerate to avenge my parents for getting on with their lives without considering my needs.

Sister Josepha looked at me with a mixture of compassion and horror, her eyelids flapping frantically at my suggestion that I become a prostitute.

I don't think she'd ever had a student speak to her so candidly, and with such passion. I felt I had nothing to lose; that she could never help me; that no one would or could rescue me—Mum had taught me that lesson a long time ago. I was still a child and saw the world in very black and white terms. In my limited experience, all I could see was the destruction of my plans to get an education and become a self-supporting professional. My future now seemed to offer nothing more than a low-paid job, or marriage and therefore reliance on a man who could support me.

For as long as I was aware, I had held onto the intention to be independent. As I was growing up, most of the women around me were housewives; it was practically mandatory.

Relinquishing their independence, they had chosen the roles of wife and mother and assumed their husband's identity, relying on him to succeed. Once you were married, you were expected to stay at home and raise a family. You couldn't get a job, or you had to leave your job once you were married. Mum had worked as a bank teller after she left school. But as soon as she married my father, she gave up her job, which was the norm in those days. She hadn't been raised to consider a career, and going to school wasn't that important. There was certainly no expectation that a woman would study at university. Despite that, education was important to her. She had worked hard to give us all a private education. She went back to school herself to study psychology. But Mum never pressured me or my sisters to achieve academically. She seemed pleased about my ambition. She was always ambitious for success and had worked in business with my father, then went on to open her own stores. But her focus was more entrepreneurial than academic.

I certainly admire women who devote their lives to their family, but success is a very personal thing. I wanted to succeed on my own terms. I didn't want to rely on anyone. I certainly didn't want a man to define me. I wanted to define myself. But as I sat in Sister Josepha's office, my clear vision of this future seemed to have been snatched away from me. I was having an identity crisis.

Sister Josepha listened to me with her eyes closed. I felt that she was praying for me and that by closing her eyes she would bring a sense of calm and peace to the room. I watched her as she prayed. I stopped talking. She opened her eyes. I could see she was distressed. I thought: Why aren't my parents similarly distressed about my crisis? Here's a woman who I barely know feeling my pain, understanding what it means to lose the opportunity to pursue an education.

Sister Josepha could see that I was angry, and that in my fragile state I was at risk of making some poor decisions. Her calm reaction put an end to my ranting. In the silence I could suddenly hear what I'd been saying. I didn't like where I was going with my plans. I was letting the situation get a hold of me. I was bending and was about to break. The last time I did that, I rolled a girl down the stairs in a rubbish bin—behaviour that I deeply regretted. I wasn't going to let this situation get the better of me.

I looked at Sister Josepha and said, 'You know what, my mother and father have had their life. This is my life now. I'm not going to let them stop me.' I was going to do it my way: my rebellion was to defy the odds stacked against me.

Sister Josepha opened her eyes and picked up the phone. She had a brief conversation that I couldn't understand. After she hung up, she said, 'We have granted you a scholarship for Year Twelve. All your books will be purchased through the library and will be on loan to you for the year. Any stationery you need will be provided.'

I couldn't believe it; she was going to help me. This was a life-changing moment. My image of a dark and hopeless future faded and my mind switched to a different channel. It was the channel I wanted—the lifestyle channel, not the horror show.

Thanks to Sister Josepha's offer, I could stay with my sisters and not have to move. I could once again pursue a university degree, a profession and independence. I was a fighter and my new call in life was to become a professional fighter.

My cousin Mara was a lawyer and she had suggested I study law rather than medicine that had difficult prerequisite subjects. All I needed was the marks to get in. I could drop chemistry, maths and physics and study subjects that I would enjoy and could excel in—legal studies, politics, art, biology and English. My year ahead was planned. My faith had been restored.

*

WHEN SHE LEFT, my mother told me that I could choose where I wanted to live. She believed that at sixteen I was old enough to be with my sisters; after all, she was married at sixteen. I don't think she realised the tremendous burden she had placed on me by granting me that freedom.

I told her that I was staying with the girls, that I had received a scholarship and was planning to study law. She agreed to let me stay.

I was probably too young to be living without parents but I felt safe with Bettina and Teresa. In a way, Bettina became our mother. She was eighteen and working with our father. She would shop, cook and pay all the bills. She was a bit of taskmaster and never allowed me to indulge in self-pity about my struggle, telling me to 'snap out of it'. In retrospect, I can see that perhaps she felt that if she was too sympathetic, it would affirm my plight and she wanted me to get through this challenge. Either that or she was in denial. The workload and the responsibility she had assumed was enough without compounding it with the truth.

Teresa was working full-time in fashion and spent a lot of her time partying; she'd be out all night and was often the last one to leave a venue. She had a huge social network, became a fixture at many nightclubs and always had somewhere to go and someone to go with; she loved her independence.

As for me: I wasn't loving it so much. These days, I probably would have ended up in foster care—though I don't think my mother would have let it get to that. She'd never have allowed me to live with someone we didn't know.

Christmas that year was really tough. It was my first Christmas without my whole family—a far cry from the

Christmases of my childhood. Ben was at Dad's and Mum spent the day with her new family. Bettina, Teresa and I celebrated with our Irish neighbours who'd become an extension of our family. My Irish sweetheart, with whom I was in a platonic relationship, made sure that I was alright. His mother had taken us under her wing and was a great support if I was ever unwell or needed advice.

I spent that summer preparing for Year Twelve, reading all my English novels and becoming familiar with my textbooks. I was a girl on a mission. I started working around the corner as a receptionist at a car yard. The two guys at the yard, both in their twenties, knew I was living with my sisters and tried to help out, always making sure I was okay and asking if I needed anything. Occasionally they'd take me out to dinner.

When I was in Year Twelve, they'd often drive past me waiting for the school bus and wave from their sports convertible. Sometimes they'd pull up and persuade me to spend the day with them. Every now and then I'd succumb, and wearing my school uniform, we'd go to the car auctions and then out for lunch.

I was always a bit wary of anyone who tried to help me, curious about their motivation. But I was beginning to learn that some people simply do things out of the goodness of their hearts. They don't necessarily want anything from you; their reward is knowing that you're okay and that they've contributed to making sure you're okay. I was starting to understand that one person can make a difference, and I resolved that one day I would be that kind of person. This boosted my determination to become a woman of substance, someone with something to give.

Many years later, I discovered that one of the guys had grown up in the house I bought with my first husband. He had shared the front bedroom with his younger brother, which then became my first son's nursery. I liked that I knew the history of the house and that good people had once lived there.

Getting through Year Twelve was a challenge without the support of my parents. It took a lot of discipline and commitment, and the journey got harder as the year progressed. I recall being angry and often thinking it was all too hard and contemplating throwing it all in, but reminded myself that it was my decision. It was an interesting rebellion. I was determined to defy the odds. I didn't want to fall through the cracks. I was determined to view my situation with a clear mind, and I saw the acquisition of knowledge as the path towards empowerment. In my current predicament, I was vulnerable and alone; but I definitely didn't want to remain gullible and naive.

I received a lot of support from the nuns and teachers at school. My class teacher, Miss Brady, would give me a wakeup call every morning at seven-thirty, letting the phone ring twice then hanging up. My art teacher, Miss Griffiths, would bring me fruit and sandwiches. She'd also bring me a needle, thread and buttons to fix my school dress that was often held together with safety pins. The students voted me class captain to encourage me to come to school every day. My friends were supportive and would invite me over for dinner because they knew I wasn't eating properly and had lost a lot of weight. Sister Josepha would call me into her office every few weeks to check on how I was coping. I was always stoic when I saw her. Firmly restrained in my distress, I didn't want her to think that she had wasted her time giving me an opportunity, or conclude that I wasn't strong enough to step up to the mark.

Every week my uncle would send a large box of fruit and vegetables. We always had apples and an endless supply of tomatoes. My staple diet became tomato on toast. The bread didn't have to be fresh but the tomatoes always were. Mum would come over and cook every now and then. I never told her that I was struggling. I didn't want her to worry. By mid-year she was heavily pregnant with my brother who was born in June. A new baby took up all her time so the visits became less frequent.

I was so excited about having a little brother. I got a phone call at school the day he was born, and that afternoon we all raced to the hospital to see Mum lying in bed with her beautiful baby boy, Oscar. Ben didn't come to the hospital. He'd heard the news, but had no-one to celebrate with, as neither my father nor his wife shared his joy. Ben felt isolated, which caused some resentment between him and my father's wife.

Ben would visit most weekends. He was really missing living at home, and being away from us and his Brighton friends was very difficult. He'd started attending a school close to Dad and had to make new friends. Looking back now, I realise how tough the move must have been for him. I've practised family law for many years and one of the paramount considerations in custody cases is the separation of siblings. Generally, the court will not separate children who have grown up together, especially if they don't want to be separated.

We'd go to Dad's house every Sunday. He paid our rent and gave Bettina a car. We'd all pile in and drive for fifty minutes to get there. Dad would always cook a roast with potatoes covered in bunches of parsley that were laced with garlic, and mountains of veal schnitzel. He made semi-dried black olives and would marinade fresh green olives in garlic and chilli. It was a feast. I loved going to visit him; the smell of his cooking was the last remnant of a childhood I cherished.

My dad lived with his wife, her daughter and Ben in a comfortable house with a swimming pool. They didn't have children together. Every time I was there I sensed the tension mounting between my father's wife and Ben. He started running away from home, spending nights away with no one knowing where he was. Often, he'd come home to Brighton and sleep on the couch. We didn't mind but it was affecting his schooling. I kept telling him that he needed to go to school, reminding him of the importance of getting an education, that when he grew up he would only have himself to rely on.

Teresa was still working in fashion, and spending a lot of time partying; she was full of energy. Bettina was less inclined to party so hard. She had a boyfriend who was now living with us. She would go to work every day while her boyfriend would stay at home and paint with Honey keeping him company. Honey became our watchdog, barking ferociously every time someone walked past the front gate. She slept next to my bed and made me feel safe, knowing that she'd alert me to any intruders. She was a great dog. Not being photogenic, she managed to ensure her raised tail and backside made it into many of our photos. We would pose for the camera, trying to model a fashion shoot, but Honey's backside would invariably be front and centre of the shot.

She also had her naughty side. She wasn't allowed to sleep on our beds but we'd come home to find her asleep on a bed with her head on the pillow and garbage strewn all the way up the corridor and in the kitchen. She'd always take a scrap of garbage and place it on the pillow under her sleeping head. Despite being punished numerous times, she persisted in this strange behaviour. We came to the conclusion that she might be a bit simple.

After Mum left I moved into her bedroom and Teresa moved into Ben's room with Rosie. Our shared bedroom became a living room which opened into the TV room. Mum returned most of the furniture when she realised I wasn't going to live with my father.

I set up a desk in my room and studied every day. I tried to be highly organised with my homework as well as making sure the washing was up to date and the house was clean. There were always people coming over and loud music playing. It was a very difficult environment for study. I needed the house to be as quiet as a library, whereas the girls were celebrating their freedom. Occasionally I'd come home to find someone sleeping in my bed—someone who'd been up all night and who'd taken my bed as soon as I left for school. It always annoyed me as it meant I'd have to wash my sheets before I could go to bed that night.

We basically had an open-house policy. If you couldn't get in through the front or back door, you could always climb in through the front window. We were never alone.

Our house became the party house of Brighton. I still meet people to this day who remember coming to our house to party.

I loved that the girls were having fun. I was trying to remain focused, which was difficult, and I couldn't wait to finish Year Twelve. While I've forgotten a lot about that year, I do remember that I grew up very quickly and learned to take responsibility for myself. The struggle of being a student with no income made me all the more determined to succeed. I never wanted to go without again. Most of the time I'd walk to school because I didn't have bus fare or wanted to save my money for food. Although the local bus driver let me on the bus for free, knowing my circumstances, I was very proud and I didn't want to ask for favours. The lady who owned the milkbar around the corner was also very kind, giving me fish and chips and burgers for dinner, refusing payment. I was really taken aback by people's generosity; I never asked anyone for anything, they just gave. I didn't ever ask Bettina or Teresa for help as I didn't want them or anyone to know that I was struggling. My father sent me ten dollars a week and I tried to make it last until the next payment. I never asked for more.

They say it takes a village to raise a child and between the nuns, the teachers, the bus drivers and the milkbar owner, everyone pulled together to help me. But despite their efforts I still didn't feel safe. I knew how vulnerable I was and I accepted their generosity reluctantly.

The nuns at school surprised me the most. My only other experience of nuns was at boarding school and I expected them all to be the same. Ten years had passed since my boarding school experience and I couldn't imagine that the culture had changed so dramatically. But it soon became apparent to me that nuns were the pioneers of women's liberation. They were the first women to be worldly, well-educated and free of the responsibilities of a husband or children. They had answered their call in life and had pursued their careers, independent of a family. Nuns had set up schools, hospitals and orphanages. They were missionaries who travelled the world, guided by their courage and conviction. They weren't sheltered and interceded for people who were in a crisis. They were open-minded and forgiving and promoted love and community. I didn't realise it at the time, but they were raising me to become a woman of substance.

I wasn't the only girl they had an impact on; the nuns nurtured many strong women at Star of the Sea. Germaine Greer attended the same school in the 1950s. The voice of the feminist movement and bestselling author of *The Female Eunuch*, Greer defined her goal as 'women's liberation' rather than 'equality with men'. In a way, she paved the path for my career in a predominantly male industry. I didn't want to be a man; I wanted to have the freedom to be a woman with the ambition and goals that had traditionally been characteristic of men. I don't necessarily agree with everything Greer said, but she was a woman with the courage to fight for what she believed in.

I had been at Star of the Sea College for five years. The students were a mix of girls—new generation Australians, mainly children of European migrants, and the children of past students. Like my parents, the migrant families wanted to provide their children with bigger and better opportunities. They had a solid work ethic and didn't brag about their wealth if they had it. The students were down-to-earth. Being an all-girls school, there were no boys to distract us. We could all be ourselves and no one seemed to judge you; my brief experience of bullying on my first day was long forgotten. I continued to have zero tolerance for bullying and would defend anyone who was teased. Often, I became friends with girls who seemed awkward or out of place and I discovered that behind the thick Coke-bottle glasses there was often a girl who was smart and hilarious. Generally, I was a pretty tough girl who was friends with everyone, had a big sense of humour and a spirit of adventure.

Though the year was often a tremendous struggle, I never told my parents how hard it was; I didn't want them to worry. Very quickly, my sisters and I learned to be streetwise.

Bettina was fierce; she had a 'take no prisoners attitude' and she knew that Dad was only a phone call away. She was learning how to run a household and how to run a business.

We had lots of friends who visited regularly. Bettina had made friends with a girl who was studying fine art at college; she seemed to socialise with a lot of creative people. One of her girlfriend's friends was a tall, dark, handsome boy that all the girls had a crush on. He was a stylish European boy with a gentle disposition, and all our girlfriends competed for his attention. He lived locally so he came around often, arriving in his 1974 mint-green Fiat 124. I remember the day I met him; he was sitting in our kitchen with Bettina and a few other people. I walked in after school wearing my school uniform, my hair in a ponytail. I had just broken up with my boyfriend so I was spending more time with my sisters and her friends. We were all curious about who he liked out of the girls. To my surprise, I soon discovered that I was the focus of his attentions.

We started going out in August of that year. Being older than I was—he was twenty-two—I hung onto him like a life-raft. He would drive me to school and pick me up; we had a lot of fun together and became great friends. He knew I was studying hard to get into law and he gave me time to study and sustained me throughout the year. He was surprised at how mature and sensible I was for my age. I was no longer afraid of being alone; for the first time in a while I felt safe. I could see that we might have a future together. The fact that I was only seventeen was not an issue for me. I didn't feel my age; I was more focused on being alright and planning my future.

Two weeks before my exams, I went to stay with my mother and her new husband. Mum hadn't stopped me from staying with the girls but she knew I needed some nurturing before my exams. It gave me an opportunity to study without the distraction of our partying household, although a crying baby was also difficult. Oscar was only a few months old and I was sleeping in his room. Mum would be up through the night nursing him and trying to keep him quiet. She would whisk him into another room to feed him and bring him back when he had settled. I had a lot of broken sleep during those weeks and felt like I was missing out on all the fun at home, but I also knew that I had to make the sacrifice. Mum drove me to my exams and my boyfriend picked me up and took me back to Mum's, who always had a delicious meal ready for me. I couldn't help feeling guilty that Bettina, Teresa and Ben weren't with me to enjoy the meal.

Mum was very happy and in love. Both she and her husband were working and studying, Mum undertaking a degree in psychology and her husband was completing his computer science course. I was really happy for her and pleased that I hadn't shown her my anger throughout the year. I didn't want that negativity to affect our relationship.

The day I finished my exams I felt liberated. School life was finally behind me. No more school dresses or ugly brown school shoes and socks. In fact, I have never worn a pair of socks or flat shoes since. I packed up my bags and didn't look back. I could now be the woman I had been training to be on the weekend. I loved fashion, like my mother and my sisters, and could wear jewellery and makeup as much as I wanted, without getting into trouble or having it confiscated. Throughout school I had been in trouble for wearing blue eyeliner and several silver rings on my fingers, but by the end of Year Twelve the teachers just let it go—after all, who were they going to report me to? They respected that I was independent and that I lived half my life as an adult.

Living on my own now felt okay; I had probably got used to it. That summer I started in a job selling imported Italian shoes at a store in the local shopping strip. Every day I dressed up in high heels and mid-length dresses. Shoulder pads were very popular then and my hair was long and curly. I wore it in an eighties quaff with big majestic earrings. Boy George from Culture Club had a big influence on fashion, as did Malcolm McLaren's 'Buffalo Girl'—full roughed skirts pulled in with big leather belts and gypsy tops. We wore shredded ribbons in our hair and ankle boots.

By this time Bettina had stopped working for Dad and bought herself a sewing machine; she loved clothes and was planning to be a fashion designer. They say that if you love your job, you will never work a day in your life. It seemed the natural thing for her to do.

*

I WAS OFFERED a place in the arts faculty at university. I couldn't believe that I had defied the odds; I had done it! Under the circumstances, I was lucky to pass Year Twelve and I hadn't expected to get into law straight away. I knew that if I worked hard, I could transfer faculties and combine arts and law. I was on my way.

On my first day at university I chose subjects knowing that they were a stepping-stone into law. I needed to achieve high grades so I enrolled in subjects that I loved, such as art history, which became my major. The course I was embarking on would qualify me as an art gallery curator. I was excited to be at university and keen to get started. I knew it would take two years to transfer, but I was willing to put in the effort and wait.

I was an enthusiastic student. I would get up early every morning and catch a bus to university. I worked part-time on the weekends in a men's clothing store and hung out with my boyfriend. He was still living at home with his mum and dad and two sisters. His parents were factory workers and they had a stable home life: very quiet and ordered. They ate dinner as a family every night at a set time and would talk at length about the meal—the cost of the tomatoes we were eating, the vegetables currently in season. It felt simple, very suburban and a bit boring, which was exactly what I needed. I would sneak into his bungalow at night and tippy-toe out in the morning. I didn't want to stay at home alone.

One morning I snuck out of the house with my hands full of clothes and ran straight into his father. The secret was out. His mother was far from impressed. She started to argue with her son about me, criticising me for not having parents at home and calling me a street kid. If only she knew how hard I had worked to never let that happen! She had no idea who I was or how much integrity I had. She was an old-fashioned and very controlling woman from Cyprus who wanted her son to marry a Cypriot girl whose parents would come over and speak Greek and talk about tomatoes. She took an immediate dislike to me. Regardless, I always tried to please her. I wanted her to know who I was. I would smile and help her with the dishes and indulge her in her excruciatingly boring conversations. She offered my boyfriend a ticket to go to Cyprus to meet another girl, a wife. I suggested he accept the ticket and that I meet him over there; I needed a holiday.

Despite her pleadings and her opposition, my boyfriend and I decided to move in together. I was eighteen and he was twenty-five. He was working full-time in an advertising company as a junior art director and had been saving money to move out of home. His father was always pleasant; he did not judge me for not having parents at home or for being Italian. He didn't want us to pay rent so he gave us a deposit to buy a house. We held off moving until settlement. His father involved me in going to open for inspections and let us choose the house we wanted. He helped us get a home loan and assisted us when we moved.

The house we chose was a small 1930s Californian bungalow in a modest suburb close by. It had brick cladding around the front that covered the weatherboards. There were three bedrooms, a large front yard and a large backyard. It had never been renovated so we had to light the hot water boiler in the bathroom for hot water. We didn't care; we were happy to be together. His mother protested by only ever coming to our house once and wiping her finger across the light switches to check if I had dusted. Fortunately, I was very house proud and vigilant about cleanliness. His father came by every weekend to do the garden; we would wake up on a Saturday morning and find him out there pruning trees. I think he was happy as long as his son was happy. He was a smiley old man who never said a bad word about anything or anyone. I liked that my boyfriend's father had such a temperament. It made me confident that my boyfriend's gentle disposition wasn't a mask of passive-aggressiveness.

I felt a bit sad leaving home as I had never been separated from Bettina and Teresa. I knew this was a permanent move and that I would probably never live with them again, so it was a significant milestone. They gave me their blessing to go. They knew I would be happy and safe.

I didn't see Bettina or Teresa very often that year. They eventually moved out of the old green weatherboard house in Brighton into a maisonette in Toorak with one of the Irish girls who'd been our neighbour. Both my sisters were working in fashion, Teresa in sales and Bettina designing and sewing clothes. Ben would come over to my house more often as he still wasn't enjoying living with Dad. Honey was still around and moved in with me. Although she was everyone's dog, at the end of the day she was mine as I had rescued her from the pet store. I loved that I had her with me; the house was so quiet. I was used to a lot of commotion, with people coming and going and parties every weekend. I was missing living with my sisters and felt sorry for Ben so I invited him to move in with us. My father approved; he was probably relieved that he no longer had to manage the dynamic between Ben and his wife.

One day Honey went missing. I searched for her for two days, ringing every dog shelter, pound and lost dogs' home. I put up flyers around the street offering a reward. I checked to see if she had made her way home to Brighton. Bettina and Teresa also kept an eye out for her. She had a way of following us around the streets and making her way back home somehow, which isn't uncommon. Apparently dogs have been known to walk for days to get back to their owners' home. Perhaps she was also missing Bettina and Teresa. I was worried that in order to get to Brighton she would need to cross a busy main road with four lanes of traffic going each way. I hoped that she'd cross safely. We had lived on the corner of a main road across the road from the beach and Honey had always been careful and seemed to be road smart.

Once she was nearly hit by a truck while playing with another dog; they had both run out in front of oncoming traffic. Bettina had seen what was about to happen and called out to her. When we wanted her to come quickly we would always say, 'Honey, chocolate!' enticing her with the promise of a treat. In a panic, Bettina screamed like a woman possessed: 'HONEY, CHOC-O-LATE!' Thankfully, it was effective and Honey bounced back onto the footpath just as the other dog was dragged under the truck and killed instantly. Maybe she wasn't so simple after all. I really hoped that Honey would use her smarts once again and return to us unscathed.

A few days later I received a call from a local council worker who had seen my flyer. He asked a few questions about Honey's appearance, including whether she had a white diamond on her forehead. I answered excitedly, sure that he'd found her, but then he broke the news that he had picked up her body a few days ago. She had been hit by a car on the main road and died.

Oh God, I was so sad, my poor little puppy gone. No-one had been there to call out to her and keep her safe. I felt guilty that I hadn't kept her locked in and that she had escaped. She had been such a part of my teenage years; how had I let this happen? We were all very sad to lose her and felt distressed about her suffering. We had all been so protective of each other and I had let Honey down. I didn't realise how much I loved her until she was gone.

A few months later I turned nineteen and got my driver's licence, albeit a year late. My father gave me an old bomb, sure that I'd dent and scratch it, promising a better car once I knew how to drive. The day before I went for my driving test, I asked Dad to take me for a driving lesson. He took me into a side street and told me to put the car in reverse and drive backwards around the block. 'Why?' I asked. In his Italian accent he said, 'If a-you can a-drive a-backwards, you can a-drive a-forwards.' I got ninety-eight per cent for my driving test.

I felt very close to my dad. I hadn't lived with him for a long time but I knew he was there for me if ever I needed him. He had never let me down, but I was a bit fragile about my family and how fractured it was, so I never asked him for anything.

I loved the freedom of having a car. I no longer had to catch buses to uni and I could drive to work. I could also visit Bettina and Teresa more often. One of the first places I drove to was the Lort Smith Animal Hospital; I wanted to adopt a dog who was about to be put down. I chose a very distressed-looking Golden Labrador cross who had kennel cough from being hosed down with cold water in his cage; I think he was about two years old. The Lort Smith Hospital has come a long way since then. I hear that they no longer put down strays but keep them in warm kennels until someone comes to adopt them.

I put the dog in the back of the warm car and he lay down on his side and slept all the way home. We named him P.S as he was a postscript of Honey. I knew from then on that I really loved dogs and that I would always have one.

Unfortunately we only had P.S for a few months. He ate snail pellets that my boyfriend's father had left in the garage and was poisoned. I rushed him to the vet but it was too late. Seeing him die really hurt me. I knew that caring for a pet was a big responsibility, but this wasn't going to stop me from caring for another one.

This time I waited a while. Years later I bought a puppy for my son, a black and white Poodle Maltese cross. We named him BooBoo but we called him 'the captain'. He was such a fantastic little dog. We bought him a companion, and named her Pepsi.

BooBoo was replaced by Ninja: a cream Labrador Poodle cross. We named him Ninja because as a puppy he was the same colour as the polished floorboards which camouflaged him. He'd disappear and then reappear exactly where you were looking. He starred on *The Real Housewives of Melbourne* and is a much-loved member of our family.

But getting back to 1984 …

Ben was still living at my place and my relationship with my boyfriend was going well. We were working on renovating our house, painting on the weekends and pulling off the brick cladding. We had settled in and started to host dinner parties and have friends over.

I completed my first year of university and was pleased with my results. The stability of my new home life had given me the opportunity to do well. But there was more going on in my life than study and my new home. My enduring love of fashion was drawing me into the fashion industry.

CHAPTER THREE

A Powerhouse
of Fashion
(1983–1998)

TERESA WAS WORKING full-time at Silitto, a clothing store in Chapel Street, South Yarra. My boyfriend and I would go to Chapel Street most Friday nights for dinner; our favourite restaurant was La Lucciola, across the road from Teresa's shop. The restaurant was owned by husband-and-wife Rosa and Sam and their sons Tim and Simon also worked there. I still go to that restaurant, which is still run by the same family whom I have now known for over thirty years.

Although we loved fashion, we didn't have a lot of clothes. We'd rummage through the local opportunity shop in search of bargains. Teresa was the best at finding great things to wear; she'd always manage to find a coat from Harrods or an Italian scarf. With her experience in fashion and her blend of new and old clothes, she always looked great. Bettina had started making her own clothes and one weekend she went to a fancy-dress party dressed as Cinderella. She'd torn up an old white sheet and splashed black paint all over it to give the impression of cinders. I had found the dress and decided to wear it one Friday night to Chapel Street, pulling it in around the waist with a thick black leather belt.

When I walked into Silitto, Teresa's boss, Joe, asked where I got my dress. I told him that Bettina had made it. He said he loved it and asked if Bettina would make him a few to sell in his shop. Of course she agreed.

With very little income, Bettina purchased a roll of fabric from a supplier in the city, Job Warehouse in Bourke Street. The warehouse was piled with metres of fabric in every colour and texture. Walking into the store was like entering a dark cave full of treasures that you had to dig deep to find. The owner never looked happy. He wasn't particularly interested in customer service, he knew that the fabric would sell itself as no-one would bother entering the shop unless they intended to buy; and he had no real competition as the fashion industry was relatively small in those days.

Bettina purchased plain cotton and delivered the dresses the following week. Within the week, they were all sold.

Joe ordered more. This time, Bettina was more creative. She bought fabric paint in various colours. Orange and blue were all the rage so she splashed different colours on the fabric. Once again, all the dresses sold. It was beginning to look like the start of something new. At the time, we had no idea that this would be the birth of the Bettina Liano brand; and of course no idea that, years later, Teresa would be inducted into the local council's hall of fame for her contribution to fashion in Melbourne. I'm still wondering where that illustrious hall is; if anyone finds it, let me know!

Things were certainly looking up. With a newfound sense of freedom, I could go anywhere, do anything and dress how I wanted. I was excited that I had worn a dress, albeit a rag, that had given Bettina an opportunity to start making clothes. It was purely by accident that her talent was discovered. She kept purchasing fabric, saving up enough money to buy her favourite colours and textures.

Her next rolls were black cotton jersey, then white cotton jersey. She would usually buy only a few metres at a time and avoided expensive components like zips and buckles, designing jersey wrap-around tops and skirts with ruffles. Her jersey range was quite basic but glamorous. Using black jersey with white trim or white jersey with black trim, she made shorts, dresses, tops and skirts. She only used pure cotton, refusing anything synthetic or any material that would pill. She tested each fabric to see if the colours ran under water or if they shrank. She didn't want the white trim to go grey. She was vigilant about quality control. It was beyond our imagination that one day she'd be commissioning her own fabric designs and buying any fabric she wanted, locally and from overseas.

Bettina set up a sewing machine in our front room—the room that had previously been my bedroom. She would sew for hours, into the night, to finish filling orders. She started making pieces for a few celebrities in the music industry. She had become close friends with the lead singer from Kids in the Kitchen, a band that was popular at the time. She became well connected in that industry and was known for her talent. Her business kept growing.

I didn't stay in contact with many of my school friends once I left school. Instead I had a lot of male friends; in fact, most of my friends were boys. It was the early eighties and there was a major shift towards gay culture; boys were coming out everywhere. One of my cousins seemed to have a knack for going out with boys who turned out to be gay; in fact, every boy she ever went out with eventually came out. She couldn't help but wonder whether she'd had anything to do with it. As the news of HIV and AIDS began to unfold, there was a shift away from the sexual revolution of the sixties and seventies towards safe sex. It was no longer about birth control, but about health and safety.

It took a lot of courage for our friends to announce their sexuality. We were open-minded and immediately accepting. Their camp humour was fun and hilarious as many of them went over the top to make a statement and publicly declare who they were. Phrases such as 'fag hag' were thrown around and landed on every girl who was single and hung out with gay boys. Teresa was definitely a 'fag hag' for a while. Being in the fashion industry, she was surrounded by boys who were flamboyant and eccentric.

Our gay friends looked out for us. Most of them were still living at home and often faced with the dreaded task of telling their parents about their sexuality. Many of them had been teased at school for not being athletic or for being effeminate. We would help them find the courage to stand up for who they were. I discovered that many gay boys had macho fathers and enjoyed close, loving relationships with their mothers. It was always a good start for them to speak to their mother. Most of them found their courage in the emerging gay liberation movement. In reality, they were stronger men than their macho fathers as they had the strength to stand up to a prejudiced and homophobic society. It was an exciting and empowering time and the nightclub scene exploded. Gay clubs opened everywhere in Melbourne, and we danced in all of them.

*

BY LATE 1984, Mum had started to talk about opening another shop, mainly for Bettina to sell her clothes. There was a shortage of fashion in Melbourne so there was room for us to start a business. Bettina was initially reluctant given that Mum had run clothing stores in the past that weren't longstanding businesses, but eventually we all agreed to go into business together.

Mum started looking for a shop to lease and we were working on a name for the store. We didn't want to stock brands that were already established; instead, we set our sights on opening a store for young designers like Bettina. Teresa was scouting around for talent at fashion design schools. We decided that the formula for the store would be exclusive clothing that was not mass-produced; we would stock items that were beautifully tailored and made with quality fabrics.

Mum suggested that we name the shop 'Bettina Liano' but Bettina would not agree. She didn't want her name to carry the responsibility of the business, nor did she want to risk tarnishing her brand if we weren't successful. Mum financed the shop, ensuring that each of us had a role in the business. We all recognised Bettina's talent and backed her all the way, hoping her days of struggle would soon be over and that we would sell enough clothes to keep the business afloat. Bettina had already been stocking a few stores in Melbourne as well as a wholesaler in Sydney. She saw the shop as an opportunity to stock a new outlet and grow her brand.

In 1985 we leased a store in Toorak village and called it Sempre L'unico, meaning 'the only one', or 'always unique'. It was a small shop in a side street with parking spaces in front and a few stylish shops on either side—a hairdressing salon owned by Lillian Frank, a French patisserie called Toorak Tarts, a beauty salon and a jewellery store. The shop was fitted out with wrought-iron tables and chairs. The palette was black and white with French grey curtains in the fitting rooms and fresh flowers on display. We managed to fill the shop with beautiful stock. By the winter of that year we were ready to trade.

Bettina had made enough money to invest in a relatively expensive over-locking machine. She had studied men's tailoring and learnt how to make jackets by hand. She would cut her own patterns and sew her own dresses. For our grand opening she had produced a stunning winter range. She loved stretch jersey because it could stretch across the body while maintaining its elegant drape. Moreover, it was comfortable and warm. Black was in fashion then, so she invested in a roll of black pure wool jersey. Her inspiration for that season was the designs of Jean Paul Gaultier.

Once Bettina completed her range, we commissioned a photo shoot to showcase all her designs. My cousin Rosie and I were the models and a friend, who was still studying photography but already proving her talent in capturing a beautiful image, took the photos. We loved working with students who had bold ambitions, like many of the designers whose clothes we stocked. Our friend went on to become the photographer for GUESS in the USA; she is still there and living her dream.

We found an old vacant mansion in Toorak and set up the shoot on the balcony, incorporating its large white columns and balustrades. The photos were mainly black and white, and we framed them using black wood with a fine edge. We used the photos to decorate the shop's walls.

Bettina worked on her logo and had labels printed. Her first logo was an image of three squares, one on top of the other, progressing from a large square at the base to smaller on top. Her name 'Bettina Liano' was next to the image. Over the years, her logo evolved. In the late eighties, she changed the squares to a circle. The 'O' branding became synonymous with her name; it was a simple symbol that everyone recognised as her design.

I was still at uni so I started working part-time in sales and admin. Teresa left her job selling imported clothing and became our full-time sales girl while Bettina was our in-house designer. Each of us had our role and we never competed with one another; we had matured into young women with our own individual style and strengths.

Our store was distinguished by a fresh approach to fashion. As mentioned previously, our mother exposed us to fashion from a very young age, involving us in her clothing stores and showing us her imported fashion magazines. Stylish and elegant as is typical of her Italian heritage, Mum had a passion for beautiful shoes, handbags, clothing and jewellery. She taught us about the quality of fabrics and the finish on a garment. Her style was eclectic and diverse, which influenced the development of our own individual styles. Mum reinvented herself constantly, moving with the trends whether it be hairstyles, makeup, shoes, fabrics and shapes. Teresa had fallen in love with her 1940s style, Bettina her tailored and bohemian style, and I was taken by her glamour. Her influence is still evident in our styles today. I certainly love glamour and have often been heard to describe myself as the ultimate drag queen.

There weren't many high-fashion clothing stores in Melbourne in the early eighties. Most of the high-fashion clothes were imports, available at a few small stores.

Most other outlets stocked locally or Chinese-made mass-produced garments that were simply clothes rather than fashion. It was difficult to find a shop that was your go-to store when you were trying to reinvent yourself—and, after all, fashion is all about reinvention.

Bettina had been associated with the Fashion Design Council of Victoria, showing her clothes in one or two parades along with many other young designers who were emerging at the time. The parades invariably drew a sell-out crowd with guests queuing in the street to get in. The FDC shows were always a great success, but there was nowhere to buy the range that was on show as there was no outlet. But this was about to change; our timing was perfect.

Bettina and Teresa went looking for designers who could capture a European sensibility. Fabrics and finishes along with limited designs were the key ingredients to the designs we were seeking; we wanted to offer our clients an exclusive range. We found some designers who were just graduating from design school, and who demonstrated a passion that was similar to ours. Through the FDC, we also sourced designers who, like Bettina, had a great talent and were just starting out. We arranged for the supply of stock by sale or return. The designers would receive a cheque every week for the garments that sold, thereby providing them with steady cash-flow and an outlet.

Stocking only the best new wave of unknown or new young designers was our guiding principle—for example, Martin Grant who launched his first ready-to-wear collection when he was sixteen. His designs were always beautifully made and sold very quickly. He went on to win Young Designer of the Year and soon after established his studio in Paris. Naomi Campbell made a surprise appearance in his first runway show, modelling his collection. This was the period of the rise of the supermodel. Apart from Campbell, there was Linda Evangelista, Christy Turlington and Cindy Crawford, to name a few. We watched intently as they graced the catwalks of the fashion runways in Paris and Italy.

The other designers we stocked—all of whom went on to build their own fashion empires—included Fiona Scanlan, Third Millennium, Jenny Bannister, Dinosaur Design jewellery, Peter Alexander sleepwear and Alannah Hill via Indigo fashion store. Melbourne was on its way to establishing itself as the fashion capital of Australia.

Through word-of-mouth, we quickly built up a strong client base. There was no social media to rely on in those days, nor did we have a budget for advertising. Nevertheless, within twelve months Sempre L'unico was trading exceptionally well. We had employed a few sales girls to help out and we were ready to expand.

In 1986 our business was doing well, and I decided to study marketing in order to learn how to successfully market our brands. I hadn't given up on law but felt that a bachelor of business would be useful. Despite it being a competitive course to get into, due to my high marks and experience, I successfully transferred to the faculty of business and studied marketing for the year, gaining valuable insights and knowledge.

The shop continued to be successful. Our list of designers grew as we constantly sourced new designers as they graduated from design school. We had a regular clientele who always purchased an item when they visited the store. We turned over our stock quickly, constantly replenishing with fresh designs, there was always something new on offer; it was difficult to leave empty-handed and they knew nothing was mass-produced, so women could wear our clothes with the confidence of knowing that they would not turn up at an event dressed the same as someone else.

Due to the combination of our different styles and taste, we managed to please most of our customers, offering something for everyone. But the one thing we had in common was an eye for quality.

In 1987 we opened a second store in Chapel Street, next door to La Lucciola; we were back in our old stomping ground. Similar to our first store, it was tiled in black and

Top right: My mother as a child (right front) when she migrated from Italy with my grandmother, aunties and uncle.

Below left: In the front yard of our bayside home, with Mum, on Ben's third birthday.

Below right: Me in Grade 1 just before we went to boarding school.

Bottom: Mum and Dad in 1970 at a black tie dinner.

Above: After kinder, in 1970, standing at the front door of our house in Brighton with Bettina, Teresa and Ben.

Left: At boarding school in 1973, on the day Teresa and I made our first holy communion.

Below: In the garden of our beach-side home in 1976 just after we moved there.

Right: In the front yard of our beachside home with Bettina, Teresa and Ben just after Dad moved out in 1979.

Below left: The day we bought Honey home in 1980. Ben is holding her after her first bath.

Bottom: In my final year of school at Star of the Sea with my school friends.

Right: Modelling for a Sempre L'Unico fashion shoot in an old mansion in Toorak, wearing an outfit from Bettina Liano's first winter range.

Below: One of the shots from a photoshoot for one of our Sempre L'Unico designers in 1990.

Left: Modelling Bettina Liano's first summer range for Sempre L'Unico in 1986.

Below: One of the promotions I was photographed for that was used in our first Sempre L'Unico fashion parade in 1986.

Above: Bettina Liano promotional card created after she branched out on her own in 1992.

Right and below: The L'Unico Bourke Street store window and interior that was featured in Vogue Interiors magazine in 1989.

Above: Lunch with Bettina, Teresa, my first husband, Hali, Dad, and my father's second wife in 1988.

Right: Behind the scenes with Teresa and Bettina during a recent newspaper photoshoot for a story about the Liano sisters.

Below: A promo card for a L'Unico parade at Chasers nightclub in 1989.

Below right: Me in 1992.

SEMPRE
L'UNICO
announces the
opening of
BETTINA LIANO
men's & women's clothing
428B Toorak Rd., Toorak Village

❧

Join us in celebrating
our opening at

CHAS4RS
386 Chapel St Sth Yarra

❧

Friday 2nd June 1989

❧

10.30pm on the mezzanine

❧

Above: On my wedding day. I was 22 and wearing a beautiful dress by Fiona Scanlan. My first husband and I posed for photographs outside the Greek church, surrounded by scaffolding.

Left: Before we were married on our first day of trading at Sempre L'Unico in 1985.

white marble with wrought-iron shop fittings, a stunning chandelier and, as a centrepiece, the largest floral arrangement we could find. Near the fitting rooms at the back, we hung a huge mirror with a wooden gold-leaf frame. The store was glamorous and opulent, and we always played loud music: Barry White, Michael Jackson or Madonna. Coincidently, all our salesgirls were brunettes who loved European designers and were driven by customer service. We were strict on the girls wearing designer shoes and expensive hosiery.

Bettina married earlier that year and was eight months pregnant when we opened the store. I remember Mum yelling at her to get off a ladder where she was hanging curtains for the fitting room. Her husband had moved into the maisonette in Toorak and Teresa had moved out to give the couple the space they needed to start married life.

Hali was born on 14 November 1988, the first baby to join our family. Mum had become a grandmother at the ripe old age of forty-two. Needless to say, she looked too young to be a grandmother and the nurses at the hospital mistook her for our sister. We were so excited to have a new addition to the family, and Hali was adorable, like a little doll. It was love at first sight.

Now that Bettina was a mother, she needed to employ more staff. She maintained her studio at home where she designed and cut patterns and fabrics, but she started outsourcing the sewing to independent machinists so she could keep the stock coming.

The flavour of Europe was making its mark on Melbourne, with the opening of more cafes, bars and bistros. The city was emerging as a style and fashion capital.

With our rise to success, we received a lot of media attention with frequent photographs and interviews appearing in the newspapers. We now turned our attention to staging our own runway shows. Our star models were usually friends or dancers who we sourced through newly emerging choreographers. Some of our models were gay friends who looked fabulous in a dress. Portia De Rossi—wife of Ellen DeGeneres—once modelled for us in a photo shoot. We would host the shows at the most popular nightclubs, choosing a venue that was the hot new place to be: the Cadillac Bar, Metro nightclub, Chasers and the Underground. Teresa was the key to all our PR and marketing. Due to her years of partying and clubbing, she had an enormous network and created the most spectacular events. Despite having minimal advertising and no social media, our brand went viral. Twenty years on, people still remember the store and have fond memories of buying clothing there.

We loved Madonna and had been influenced by her launch onto the nightclub scene. Matt-red lipstick, curly hair and heavy eyebrows were the rage. Nevertheless, we avoided music that was too mainstream. Like our taste in fashion, we always sought out cutting-edge music to create the mood for our shows, such as Run-DMC, Public Enemy and the Beastie Boys. Disco was out and the rappers were in; hip-hop music was taking over.

Despite being caught up in the success of our business, I never took my eye off my ultimate goal of studying law. I was about to complete a bachelor of business in marketing so the time had come to apply for law school. It was important that I applied as an undergraduate rather than a postgraduate student, which would have required me to apply through the public system, and therefore compete with the whole of Victoria not just students at the same university. So I needed to be strategic.

Before I graduated from marketing, I walked over to the law faculty, filled in the necessary paper work and applied for a transfer to law. Shortly afterwards, I was invited to an interview with the dean of the school, Professor Louis Waller. I left the interview anxious about what the future would bring. The next student intake was after the summer break so I had no choice but to simply wait. So I waited, and waited, and waited.

One afternoon I was working in the shop when I received a phone call from Professor Waller. I held my breath as he started to speak about my application. I had achieved high distinctions in most of my subjects and he knew how much I wanted to study law and that my journey had been difficult. With much enthusiasm he said, 'Congratulations, you have been accepted into law.' Bingo! I was in.

Finally, all the years of hard work were justified. Although I'm generally not a very excitable person, on this occasion there are no other words to describe my feelings: I was over the moon. Thank you Sister Josepha, thank you to all who supported and encouraged me to finish school. My plan and my dream had been realised. My true identity was about to unfold.

Mum was thrilled; she cried and hugged me when I told her. It had taken her this long to believe that I had really meant it. I couldn't wait to start. Studying law was no longer an act of defiance or rebellion; it was a goal that I deeply wanted, one that offered a real opportunity to become the educated and fiercely independent woman I had always envisaged I would be.

By this time I was twenty-one years old, and already felt that I had been around the block one hundred times, receiving most of my education from the university of hard knocks. I had been living on my own for five years, I had completed two degrees, I was a qualified art gallery curator, I had bought and sold a home and was onto my second property. I had a successful business, I had become an aunty ... and I had thought that having four children at age twenty-one, as my mother had done, was an achievement.

I didn't have a stop button. I was never 'about to do' anything; I was always just doing it. I was running my own race, and with the focus it took to remain determined, I didn't have time to peer around to see what anyone else was doing. I was never competitive; I looked to others for inspiration so I never felt jealous. Some might have interpreted my intense focus as arrogance or self-absorption; but I was simply an accelerator who didn't want anyone around me to be the brake. I didn't feel arrogant; in fact, I felt humbled by my journey. I was fully aware that I had a lot of hard work ahead of me.

✳

IN 1988 I started my law degree, thrilled to be embarking on my career. My first day of uni was satisfying and daunting. I enrolled in five law subjects and purchased all my textbooks. Some of the books were thicker than a telephone directory with pages that were paper-thin and covered in tiny writing. There was no mucking around when they resolved to cram a truckload of information into one book!

I managed to squeeze all my lectures into four days, as I had in the past, and I worked in the stores for the balance of the week. With our ongoing success we expanded our business and opened a third store in Melbourne's CBD.

We found a store at the 'groovy' end of Bourke Street, away from all the mainstream department stores, and set up shop across the road from Pellegrini's, a cafe that was, and still is, a Melbourne institution. Having opened in 1954, Pellegrini's was one of the first espresso bars in Melbourne. Thirty-odd years later, they were still speaking Italian and hadn't changed the décor or even some of the staff. Even today, it remains the same.

Our clothing maintained its identity as cutting-edge fashion that was constantly evolving. Our suppliers had grown to some thirty designers, with a queue of hopefuls waiting to get their foot in the door. Designers knew that if they could get their range into our stores, there was no better endorsement in Melbourne and they'd be on their way to success. Bettina, Teresa and I were likened to the Fendi sisters—five sisters in Italy who, in 1946, brought a new wave of energy and enthusiasm to the House of Fendi which their parents had launched in 1925. It was the ultimate compliment for three Italian girls who had worked hard and found their passion in fashion. Appearing in magazines and newspapers, our fashion parades drawing enormous crowds each season, we had created a fashion storm in Melbourne.

Looking back, we were extremely resourceful and visionary women who were not afraid to step out and make things work. We knew the world was bigger than Melbourne but loved being part of its growing international culture and the excitement of the city's new direction. The eighties was a boom-time; we had recovered from the recession of the 1970s and this decade was marked by social and economic growth. We discovered that along with music, the economy is also a powerful influence on fashion. In times of wealth, women tend to buy colour, whereas when the economy is strained, women prefer more basic tones like black and white. By the late eighties, fashion was all about expensive clothes and fashion accessories: handbags, shoes, large gold earrings, pearl necklaces and diamantes. Hair was big, curly and bouffant with heavy makeup and bright eye shadow. Sound familiar? I often say that the eighties were my formative years. Now you can see where I'm coming from.

The aim was to dress in a style that spoke of wealth and success. Bettina created beautiful dresses with ostrich-feather hemlines, satin and fringes. High heels, usually black suede, were the go, but so were multi-coloured shoes in vivid colours. Short, tight skirts were also popular, influenced by the emerging hip-hop culture. The key word for fashion then was 'plush'.

Bettina designed the interior of the new store with white marble, silver satin fabrics and fringing on all the dressing room curtains and counter edges. We placed our signature grand floral arrangement in the middle of the room with smaller bunches of flowers on each counter. Loud music once again set the mood, usually Billie Holiday and Ella Fitzgerald or the Gypsy Kings. Our store was photographed for interior design magazines and we regularly appeared in the papers, our name and image out there for the entire world to see.

One day I opened the mail to find a handwritten letter from Sister Josepha. Dated 30 May 1988, the letter read:

> *Dear Gina,*
>
> *I saw your photo in* The Age *on Wednesday last, with Bettina and Teresa, and wanted to let you know I am delighted you are doing so well. Even though I do not think I shall be wearing any of your gear (!) I do congratulate you on your initiative and expertise in managing such a creative enterprise.*
>
> *Your photo decorated our staff noticeboard for three days and created considerable interest for your former teachers.*
>
> *It doesn't matter now, does it, if you wear five rings on one hand and three on the other—remember?*
>
> *Anyhow, I am very pleased things are going so well for you. You are not forgotten at Star [of the Sea] and you will always have a special place in my heart, Gina!*
>
> *Affectionately*
> *Sr Josepha*

There she was again, encouraging me on my journey; what a beautiful woman. I never saw Sister Josepha after I left school. I was young and keen to leave those years behind me. Naively, I thought she'd be around forever and I always planned to go and see her one day. Unfortunately, that day never came. Sister Josepha passed away before I got a chance to visit her. I did send her a letter after I finished Year Twelve, thanking her for everything she had done for me. I was pleased that along the way I had achieved my goals and had been successful. I knew she took pride in the fact that she had given me a great opportunity to finish Year Twelve and remain with my sisters. I'm sure that I wrote to let her know that I was accepted into law, but I can't recall whether I replied to her letter.

In 2014 I was invited back to Star of the Sea by the Past Students' Association who asked me to deliver a speech about my time at the school. I specifically requested that certain teachers attend as guests as I hadn't seen most of them since I left school. I was happy to discover that many of them still teach at Star all these years later. I don't know whether they were aware of how they had sustained me, and the extent of their impact on my life. Those formative years provided the foundation for who I am today.

I was warmly welcomed by an audience of two-hundred-and-fifty people. Many students from my year came along as well as current students and staff. I spoke about my final year at school and my struggle to complete Year Twelve, as well as what I had achieved since then. My children and their partners came, as did my current partner, his mother and his gorgeous daughter. One of the cast members from *The Real Housewives of Melbourne* also attended and was so moved by the experience that she told me she'd like to come back as a Catholic in her next life.

*

BACK TO THE mid-eighties ... Melbourne was prospering and there was a growing sense of excitement in the city. Most of our friends of similar age had graduated from school during this period of economic growth and were optimistic about the future. We knew that we could make it if we tried; the opportunities were out there, and we were living proof of what could be achieved. Our friends were landing well-paid jobs, banks were loaning money on houses and credit cards. We were rich!

Between working and studying, I renovated my first home—painting, polishing floorboards and pulling off the brick cladding under a cloud of asbestos dust. I had no idea what I was doing, or the possible consequences. But in the end I sold the house for a good price.

Bettina's designs were going from strength to strength. Her husband was becoming more involved in the business to help her through motherhood. Her staff had grown as fast as her finances. She was still working from her home studio and making plans to set up a warehouse studio to house her growing staff and production line.

Teresa had met her partner, Peter, with whom she's still in a relationship today. They met accidentally in front of La Lucciola, next door to our shop. I don't know exactly what happened, but Teresa went missing for a few weeks, then turned up in love with a very handsome man by her side. He was, and still is, a very talented artist. No doubt she was attracted to his artistic flair and his good looks; also his calm and even-tempered personality. In 1995 they had a son, Orson, who's now a tall handsome man with a similar personality to his father and a great sense of humour.

At the end of 1989, Melbourne was hit by a recession. We had relied on tourism for passing trade in our Bourke Street store, but a pilot strike had a particularly bad impact on that shop. As a result of the dispute, which began in August 1989, Melbourne's central business district became very quiet and many people lost their jobs. The downturn cast a shadow over our optimistic outlook and we decided to gear down for a while.

Bettina was getting itchy feet to set out on her own and launch the Bettina Liano label. Many of the designers we'd nurtured and encouraged had already branched out and opened stores to house their brands. Now they were up there amongst the world's best. In five years, we'd revolutionised the Australian fashion scene.

When Bettina created the Bettina Liano label, we decided to close the Bourke Street store. We were still trading in Chapel Street and had closed our Toorak store in 1988. Despite the recession, it wasn't long before Bettina's label was doing exceptionally well. Her clients were young women who had a disposable income—no children, no mortgage, just working to get by and to look good. They were loyal customers and enthusiastically followed her style from season to season.

Bettina had started working on a jeans range—velvet exposed button-up jeans with an extremely flattering fit. She produced a large range of coloured velvet including grey, burgundy, green, navy and black. I had never seen anyone's backside look so good in a pair of jeans, and evidently the whole nation agreed. By late 1989 Bettina had opened her first Bettina Liano store in Chapel Street. She went into business with her husband and manufactured the most coveted jeans Australia had ever seen; she truly was the jeans queen of Australia.

Her first store was a modern shop down the road from Sempre L'unico. The interior was very different from the interiors she had previously designed. This time, the look was more rustic, no chandeliers or wrought-iron. She was establishing her own identity as a trader. She only stocked her own label, supplemented by a few accessories from other designers. She launched her first range of jeans at that store, having sourced a specialist jeans supplier to manufacture the range. The rest of her range was produced off-site with all patterns made and cut back-of-house, where she had set up a studio and office.

Bettina was now working out of a warehouse behind her new store. This gave her the opportunity to accommodate her growing business and expand her staff; it also meant that she was no longer working from home, thereby eliminating any safety risks to Hali.

Teresa decided to work with Bettina in Bettina's new store but I continued to work at Sempre L'unico with Mum. Mum was becoming more hands-on in the business now that Bettina had branched out and I knew I wouldn't be in fashion forever. I planned to practise law as soon as I finished my degree. At the end of the day, it was really Mum's business and she kept it going until 1995.

Teresa worked with Bettina until 1992 when Bettina moved her store to a new site across the road from Sempre L'unico, where she traded until 2013. She expanded her retail outlets throughout Australia, opening her first Sydney store in 1995 and then she moved internationally to New York. She had another daughter, Olympia, in 1991. Both girls are now grown up and as enthusiastic about fashion as we were. Hali lives in New York where she set up a shop called Broadmeadows. I can see history repeating itself.

Teresa started her own fashion range in 1992, producing handbags and knitwear. She was also working as a stylist, styling high-profile celebrities such as John Farnham and Kate Ceberano, as well as being a fashion consultant to many wealthy businesswomen. In 1998 she opened her own store, launching her T.L Wood label. She had found her niche in the market with her beautiful designs, and soon became well known for her luxurious fabrics, elegant style and exemplary quality. Her style was still heavily influenced by the 1940s, showcased by my mother when it made a revival in the 1970s; her clothes were classic and sophisticated, typified by flowing fabrics and beautifully tailored jackets in sumptuous colours. Her signature pieces were knitwear in stunning mercerised cottons and silks, her palette rich and lustrous with expensive components such as braids, tassels, cords and button details. Teresa was in retail until 2014.

Bettina's designs were raunchier than Teresa's, made for girls with great bodies. Her tailoring was exceptional and she delivered garments that were feminine and sexy. She received an overwhelming response in the media and was awarded endless accolades in recognition of her immense talent. It seemed at one time or another, everyone in Melbourne owned a pair of her jeans or an item of her clothing—and if not, they aspired to. She attained a level of success that one could only dream of; she epitomised the rags to riches story—even literally, as her first dress was an old sheet!

Looking back, it's hard to believe what we achieved in such a short period of time, and trading only six days a week. Sunday trading only began in 1991 and it wasn't deregulated until 1996. Prior to that, trading on Sunday was prohibited. In fact, an Australian businessman named Penhalluriack was fined over half a million dollars in the early eighties for opening his hardware store in Caulfield. We weren't about to embark on such an expensive exercise! He appealed against his fines and led a campaign against restricted trading outside of legislated times. His actions eventually revised retail trading laws in Victoria, and with that came Sunday trading. Melbourne certainly had been a sleepy town, to some degree, but all that had changed by 1991 and the city saw a retail explosion, with customers keen to buy every day of the week.

Our mother's influence had paid off. Due to her, we had all developed an eye for fashion that started in childhood and endured into adult life. It formed the foundation of who we were, and who we continue to be. First impressions count for a lot, you don't get a second chance at first impressions and the clothes you wear are a significant factor. We wanted every woman in Melbourne to look and feel her best at all times. Feeling good and looking good is half the battle; the rest follows from there.

I remained in the fashion industry until 1998, working between Sempre L'unico and Bettina Liano's stores. Even when I started working as a lawyer, I never really left fashion. I have remained involved because of my love of it, and through Bettina and Teresa.

CHAPTER FOUR

My Husbands, My Sons and Motherhood (1988–2015)

Having lived with my boyfriend for a couple of years, at the ripe old age of twenty-one I decided it was time to get married. I chose a beautiful large diamond ring with three individual diamonds surrounded by smaller diamonds. My husband-to-be was twenty-eight and not that keen to get married, but in those days it was my way or the highway. Maybe not a lot has changed—I'm still sure about what I want and equally sure about what I don't want. You don't have to be right or wrong as long as you're certain. But as certain as I was, I've since discovered that sometimes the perfect ingredient for ruining a good relationship is wedding cake.

I remember having cold feet. My friends made light of my apprehension by suggesting they buy me slippers as a wedding present. My fiancé and I didn't have an engagement; it was too difficult with a mother-in-law who had not given her blessing and wasn't willing to attend, though we knew she'd come to the wedding.

Was I in love with him? I don't really know. I certainly did love him; he was like a brother to me and I felt safe with him. According to my thinking at the time, he had given me no reason to leave, and we had unfinished business so I stayed.

Before I committed, I did think about my Irish friend and our long-term plan to get married one day. I wanted to make sure that I was about to marry the man who loved me the most and who I loved even more. I did ask my Irish friend if he was okay about me getting married. Reluctantly, he gave me his blessing, knowing that he couldn't offer me the same things, nor the security of marriage. He was only twenty and had a long way to go before he could catch up with my fiancé. I did love him so his blessing was important.

As it turned out, my Irish friend refused to come to the wedding and suffered a degree of sadness at my decision. He eventually moved to Scotland. I stayed in contact with him and his family, but I only ever saw him again sporadically. He's now in his forties and never married, which I'm sure has nothing to do with me as our childhood was a very long time ago.

Just before our marriage, my fiancé and I bought another house in Brighton, albeit in the furthest street from the beach. Ultimately, I wanted to live as close to the beach as possible, in the street in which I grew up, but I knew it would take time to get there. Nevertheless, it was my mission. I love setting goals; it gives me drive and purpose.

Our new house was a weatherboard federation-style home. It needed renovating, which I viewed as a positive because I could capitalise on the investment. Furthermore, it was situated on a good-sized block of land, which felt right given that we were planning to have a family.

We soon embarked on our renovations and preparations for the wedding. I had completed my first year of law and I decided to defer my studies so I could focus on my wedding and on the fashion business.

The fourteenth of January 1989 was an overwhelmingly hot day. I had been preparing for this day for months— although in truth, I'd been gearing up for this wedding my whole life. Like most girls, I had contemplated my wedding day since childhood, wondering who I would marry, what he'd look like, what kind of man he would be.

Finally, there I was, a bride at twenty-two wearing a beautiful wedding dress custom-made by Fiona Scanlan, with gold ribbon, seed pearls and pearl buttons. It was made of duchess silk satin, off-white with a sheer veil and a tiara of fresh miniature roses in my hair. On my feet were satin pointy high-heeled shoes and my ears were adorned with pearl earrings. Something old, my mother's earrings; something new, the dress; something borrowed, my clutch bag; and something blue, the ribbon in my garter belt. I had a beautiful bouquet of pink peony roses to carry down the aisle.

My father was waiting anxiously as I arrived, fashionably late, and hot and bothered given my limousine did not turn up and I was forced to travel in a friend's car which had a faulty air-conditioner that blew hot air.

When I arrived at the church I was disappointed to discover that the entry and façade were covered in scaffolding; it was technically a construction site. I tiptoed over some wood and ducked under makeshift platforms where tradesmen had been working, as my father greeted me at the church door. He cupped his arm around mine and walked me down the aisle.

We were married in an old Greek Orthodox church. I was Catholic but not practising so I thought I'd go along with the Orthodox tradition. The entire ceremony was spoken in Greek. I didn't understand a word but I was there to be married, so I was happy.

We walked down the aisle as husband and wife and posed for photographs on the steps of the church beneath the scaffolding. I was sure my beautiful wedding dress was not designed for such a terrible backdrop; regardless, I was now a wife.

We celebrated at Ripponlea Estate, an old Romanesque heritage property under the care of the National Trust. The home was built in 1868 and is set on beautiful grounds with a grand Hollywood-style swimming pool and a long pebble-stone driveway. Aside from the heat, I felt like a princess. The reception was held in the grand ballroom which was adorned with fairy lights, a long bridal table and flowers everywhere. Catering was by Peter Rowland.

It was the first time my mother had seen my father since their separation, which made things rather awkward but they made the sacrifice to be there. My father came with his wife whereas my mother attended alone, bringing my little brother Oscar, who was the pageboy. It was also the first time my parents had met my in-laws as my mother-in-law had refused to meet my parents. I don't think she smiled once all day. I looked at her and thought, Okay, we get it, you're not happy. I had tried to please her by getting married in a Greek Orthodox church; I had invited all her family and friends, many of whom I'd never met, who were growing hair out of places that I had never thought possible—and that was the women. My husband laughed at my humour; he agreed that some of his mother's friends were a bit scary-looking. Eventually I realised that my mother-in-law was never going to be happy, no matter how hard I tried, so I focussed on the wedding. Sometimes the less you care, the happier you will be.

We hosted one-hundred-and-fifty guests—not a large wedding by European standards. It was elegant and glamorous, exactly what I wanted. We played jazz, Greek music, and Kate Ceberano sang with a live band as we danced the night away. Kate was one of the celebrities we'd been dressing; Bettina Liano was amongst her favourite labels.

The next day my husband and I stayed at home, hosting friends and relatives who visited while we unwrapped presents. We decided to go on our honeymoon the following year as we preferred to spend our money renovating our house.

After months of renovations, we finally had a very comfortable new home. We had knocked out walls and replaced glass doors and fireplaces, installed new carpet, new curtains, fresh paint and a nursery for a baby. A few months later I was pregnant. The anticipated honeymoon was now off the agenda, but I didn't mind: I was excited at the prospect of being a mother.

Pregnancy was an interesting experience. I was twenty-three and had always had a slim, toned body and was full of energy. I hadn't slept during the day since I was a child and could never understand the need for an afternoon nap. I was working every day with Bettina and Teresa. But for the first time in a long while I struggled to get out of bed. Morning sickness can be very debilitating. I worked out that if I ate something as soon as I got up, the nausea would subside. Then I worked out that after eating I needed a rest. So the cycle of sleeping and eating and sleeping again started. Most days I would go to work and at some point fall asleep, virtually standing up. I vowed to never be overweight as I struggled to get in and out of the car. By the end of my pregnancy I just gave up; one day I lay down on the floor and after a few failed attempts at rolling around, I stayed there for hours waiting for my husband to get home so he could help me up.

Despite my rotund physique I still managed to wear high heels, choosing the most comfortable pair of Robert Clergerie's I could find; he was the Louboutin of the eighties. These days his shoes look a bit orthopedic but still beautiful quality.

I was a bit anxious about having a baby, as most women are. Apart from a second cousin, Hali was the only baby in our immediate family. I knew that Bettina would guide me through motherhood if I needed her help, but it was the birth I was nervous about. I had accompanied my cousin Mara during the delivery of her daughter Alexandra the year before. In hindsight, I'm not sure whether witnessing this birth was a good or a bad thing. It certainly looked very painful.

I was told all manner of horror stories—about endless hours of labour, the number of stitches, the agony; stories of stillborns, deformities, blood transfusions, death ... Eventually I learned to ignore the things I didn't want to hear. I was a bit nervous, feeling as though I was sitting on a time bomb, but I knew I'd be fine and if not I'd deal with whatever unfolded as it happened.

Christos was born three weeks early on Sunday 13 May 1990, which happened to be Mother's Day. What an amazing Mother's Day gift! I was thrilled to have a son, although it didn't matter to me whether the baby was a boy or a girl. I just knew that he was a gift, the best gift I could ever receive, and that I felt love that I had never experienced before.

I wrapped him in white blankets and a little white cotton nightie and took him home a week after he was born. I had turned twenty-four in hospital, five days after his birth. He had been in the nursery with jaundice and I hadn't been allowed to nurse him. When the nurses discovered it was my birthday, they asked me what I wanted. I said I wanted my baby. Later that day they wheeled him in with helium balloons attached to his cot, singing happy birthday. It was the best birthday present ever. I promised him that I would be a good mother, that I would always look after him and that I would never leave him.

I took Christos everywhere with me, packing his little capsule in and out of the car and placing his bassinette beside me when we slept. He smelt divine, like newborn babies do. I was so protective of him, nursing and burping him for hours. One day, as I was sitting on the couch feeding him, I sat him up to burp him when I noticed brown fluid seeping from his ear. I was immediately worried. He was looking a bit floppy, as newborns do when they become inebriated with milk, and cross-eyed with wind. Panicking, I grabbed the phone and dialled the number to the hospital to consult with a nurse.

'There's something wrong,' I said, 'the baby's got fluid coming out of his ear and it's running down his face!' As I spoke, I lay Christos on his pillow and realised that the fluid I'd noticed was also down his leg, seeping through his jumpsuit. Suddenly it dawned on me that his nappy was so full that when I sat him up to burp him, it had spilled out the side and I had laid his head in the puddle of spill. Slowly I said, 'Umm … I think I've worked it out.' The nurse laughed and reassured me that it was better to call any time I was worried. My goodness, what an ordeal! From then on, I always changed Christos's nappy before I fed him. It made more sense anyway, rather than disturbing him after a feed when he was settled. These were the things I needed to work out along the way. It was going to be a quick learning curve with not much room for error.

I remember packing away the little nighties he'd worn from the hospital once he outgrew them. I pressed them up to my nose, smelled them and kissed them as I placed each one into a storage box. Christos was, and still is, my favourite person in the world—along with my other son, whom I'll get to later!

I enjoyed every day that I was home with Christos. I would hum to him when he went to sleep, usually the tune of 'Amazing Grace', and I would play music to settle him. He loved Roberta Flack and would fall sleep within minutes of her singing. We became very attached and I knew it would be difficult to leave him when it was time for me to go back to work.

By Christmas that year I was back working at the shop part-time on Friday nights and on the weekends. I would express milk so my husband could feed him in my absence. Christos was generally an easy baby to settle but he did give his father a hard time. He would cry from the moment I left until the time I got home … and then the baby would start. No, not really; only the baby would cry. His father didn't like changing nappies so he would drive all the way to South Yarra from Brighton so I could change Christos's nappy.

It was a bit hopeless of him but I enjoyed the excuse to see my little boy.

His father babysat him most weekends and would spend hours teaching him to say 'dada'. It's funny how parents compete for that first word. Dad won the competition but I knew no-one was ever going to replace Mum and it was only a matter of time before I taught him.

The following year I returned to uni, employing one of my cousins to nanny Christos. She adored him and he adored her, which gave me the confidence to concentrate on my studies. I hated leaving him; I missed him terribly and was always in a hurry to get home. I started to become increasingly anxious about leaving him until one day I suffered an awful episode of separation anxiety. I was sitting in a lecture and felt like I couldn't breathe, my pulse was racing. I ran to my car and drove straight to the doctor's, sure that something was wrong.

The doctor worked me out pretty quickly. He inquired about my home life. I told him things had been great. I was enjoying motherhood but hated leaving my baby. He asked how my marriage was going and I told him that my in-laws had been overseas for a few months, allowing my husband and I to enjoy some quality time without the tension of an interfering mother-in-law. But now my in-laws were back and things were stressful again. My mother-in-law was making my life miserable, constantly criticising me and insulting me in Greek. It was putting an enormous strain on our marriage.

My doctor—who was rather odd, it must be said—suggested that I was suffering anxiety and unless I changed something my health would suffer. So perhaps it was time to leave the marriage. Then he went on to tell me that men should not marry one woman, but instead have a 'hurum'.

'What?' I asked, confused. 'Do you mean harem?'

'Yes, a hurum,' he confirmed.

It was strange, he didn't have an accent but seemed unable to pronounce this word correctly. Anyway, I left his rooms thinking that he might be a bit of a freak, but I still pondered his advice that perhaps the marriage was not working, not because I wasn't getting along with my husband, but because the stress of my in-laws was bringing me down and undermining my sense of peace.

I stopped going to my in-law's house, hoping to avoid this negativity. But unfortunately this plan backfired. Every time we were invited, I would end up arguing with my husband because I refused to go. I was feeling increasingly anxious each time I left Christos, and my fragility made me want to avoid any situation that might exacerbate my stress. I kept replaying in the back of my mind the story my grandmother once told me about her son who'd died from diphtheria when he was twelve months old.

She'd taken him to the doctor who'd told her that she should take him home as he was dying. So she took her baby home and held him while all the women in her village gathered around, telling her that as long as he remained in her arms, he'd try to hang on, pleading with her for help. Seeing that her son was struggling, my grandmother handed her baby to a neighbour and he died as she walked away. What a terrible story. Why did anyone tell me that story? It was so distressing, and was now causing me endless anxiety.

I was disappointed that I wasn't coping with my mother-in-law and that the relationship had caused such tension in my marriage. I had known my husband for a long time and he was a good man. I could feel myself withdrawing and he was becoming more and more distant. He started to look at me as though he hated me. I felt as if I was caught in a rip, the tide taking me further and further away. I couldn't seem to swim out of it.

Eventually in October 1991 my husband and I decided to separate. Christos was eighteen months old. He didn't like not having his father around, but I tried to compensate by making sure that he saw his dad regularly. Our separation was difficult but not acrimonious. We settled our property by consent and never went to court. He was very fair in the settlement and never suggested that Christos live with him. He knew that I was a devoted, loving mother and that his son would be well looked after. He always paid maintenance and spent time with his son, although the frequency of their contact dissipated as the years went on.

My ex-husband eventually remarried and became tied up with his new family. His wife is a wonderful woman with whom I get on very well, and together they have two lovely daughters. Perhaps my ex appreciated where I had come from; he had witnessed my struggle and didn't want to add further chapters to that particular book. When his father passed away years later, I sent him my condolences and told him that his father had been a good man. I thanked him for the years we'd spent together, and for looking after me when I was a young girl.

Soon after my separation, at age twenty-five, I met a man who would become my second husband. He was living with a friend of mine and had moved to Melbourne from Sydney, although he was originally from Melbourne. He was twenty-seven. We became best friends before we started dating and fell in love, as friends sometimes do. Christos and I moved in with him after I sold my house and settled the legal affairs with my ex-husband. I was still working at the shop and studying law; I had a lot on my plate.

My new man wasn't quite as high energy as I was. He was struggling to find work and wasn't as stable financially, but this didn't bother me. I was happy to be going out with someone whom I loved and who was good to my son. He was very accepting of my past, appreciating that the older you get, the more complicated your history. He was the first man to ever tell me that I was pretty. I liked the word; it was gentle. It's not that I had never been complimented; I had received compliments before, and you know a compliment is never wasted on me: I go to a lot of effort. It was more that the word was not aggressive, it was sweet. In fact, he was a very sweet man, which I needed to balance the hard life I'd been living. I was always so tough on myself, so it made for a nice change. What I wanted now was peace. I would study for hours at night so that I could work during the day. He seemed to understand my pace despite not travelling at the same speed, which suited me at the time. I needed to learn how to pace myself, so he was a good stabiliser.

We lived together in his rented Victorian house in South Yarra while I was looking to buy another home. I brought all my furniture with me and furnished his house with large gold mirrors, paintings, Persian rugs, cream upholstered couches, lamps, tables, ornaments and a cot. There were three bedrooms and we set up the second bedroom as a nursery. Christos would sneak out of his room every night, run down the dark Victorian corridor into my room and jump into bed with me. He learned how to be very quiet when he discovered that if he woke me I would get up and put him back to bed in his room. Most mornings I would wake up and not be able to lift my head off the pillow because he would be asleep on my hair.

I employed a nanny to look after him during the day while I was at uni and at work. She was a Greek girl with a very heavy accent. Her name was Toula. Christos struggled with her name, usually calling her Toilet.

A year later I found a house to buy in Brighton and I moved in with Christos on my own; I wasn't ready to be in a long-term domestic relationship. I had saved enough money from my divorce to put a deposit on the house and was keen to get back into the property market.

My partner and I separated for about six months but remained in contact. He eventually moved in, we were still in love and there was a lot of chemistry between us; but like a lot of passionate relationships, there were regular bouts of separation and reconciliation. Eventually, after quite a rollercoaster ride, we were married in 1996. I was thirty years old and six months pregnant. We were still living in the house I had bought out of my property settlement.

By 1996, while still pregnant, I had completed my law degree and was embarking on twelve months of practical training as an articled clerk, which is required in Victoria after graduation in order to be admitted to practice as a lawyer. Mum had closed Sempre L'unico the previous year and although I worked on the odd occasion with Bettina, I had moved away from fashion now that I was focused on becoming a lawyer.

I planned my second wedding to be a low-key affair. I saw it simply as an exchange of vows to legalise our relationship and provide security to Christos—even though marriage is certainly no guarantee. We decided to hold it in the gardens with a celebrant and two witnesses, Teresa and the best man. I didn't want to get married in the registry office, which felt a bit unromantic, nor did I want to marry in a church given I was six months pregnant and divorced.

Despite my hope to keep it simple, the guest list grew. My new mother-in-law wanted to attend so she flew down from Sydney. Teresa brought Peter and Orson; and Ben, who'd studied photography, came to take photos. Bettina turned up unexpectedly with her two girls who were carrying baskets of rose petals. Like a typical five-year-old, Christos was running in a state of hyperactivity and excitement. My father and his wife came to give us their blessing and to take us all to lunch after the exchange of vows. Mum didn't come because Dad was there.

I had been reluctant to get married. Our relationship had been unstable and I knew getting married was no guarantee that we would stay together forever. At least it was a plan and that felt better.

In the end, it turned out to be more romantic than I had anticipated. Despite me not wearing a wedding dress, there was no question that this was a wedding. Everyone was so happy. My partner and I had certainly had our ups and downs but now there was a feeling of peace between us. The relationship felt stable and we had made a public declaration of our love for each other.

My second son Myles was born on Sunday 16 September 1996, three weeks early just like his brother, but this time it was on Father's Day. Clearly, both my sons wanted to make a statement. Myles was, and still is, a beautiful boy like his older brother—and, of course, one of my favourite people in the world.

Christos, who had placed his order for a brother very early in my pregnancy, was so excited about Myles's arrival. For some reason, he wanted to call him 'stripy', which sounded like 'shtripy' when he said it. He had a very cute way of pronouncing words. Sometimes we'd play 'I spy with my little eye'. Christos would say, 'Something beginning with "ch"'. I'd look around and say 'chair', which was wrong, then 'church', which was also wrong. Eventually, I'd give up and he'd pronounce: 'Chrees!' He meant trees.

Before the birth I asked him what he would call the baby if it were a girl. He said, 'Mum, if it's a girl I think you should leave her at the hospital; someone will want her.'

'But I'm a girl,' I said. 'What if my mum had left me at the hospital?'

He thought about this for a minute, then agreed that maybe we should bring her home anyway.

The brothers bonded instantly. Christos would run if Myles needed a fresh nappy and would cry if Myles was ill. Myles in turn adored Christos, always laughing and smiling at him. One of his first words was 'Didi' for Christos. Later he pronounced it 'Disdos'. The two boys have always been kind to each other and looked out for each other. You couldn't give Myles a biscuit without him extending his other hand saying, 'One for my brother.'

Myles was a divine little boy just like his brother. But unlike his dark-haired, brown-eyed brother, he was blond with blue eyes. I referred to the two of them as salt and pepper. Myles resembled the doll I received as a girl one Christmas morning that I called Nylon; he also smelt like her, so his nickname became Nylon. He was a happy baby, very affectionate, always smiling and easy to settle. When we sang to him he'd look at us with delight. He took his time learning to walk, always careful about falling over. He developed a funny little laugh when he was about to hurt himself; Christos and I described it as the death laugh. The greater the danger, the harder he laughed—something we worked out one day when he was climbing out of his high chair and started laughing hysterically just as he was about to fall. We seemed to be able to find humour in most situations.

Occasionally, when the Italian mother in me comes out, they find it amusing. In fact, they've made it virtually impossible to parent them without humour getting in the way of discipline. I let my boys make fun of situations as long as they aren't being disrespectful. I have parented them through leading by example and never expect anything from them that I haven't demonstrated myself. I am always very patient and caring towards them, which is how I've taught them what love means. If a child comes from an abusive home in which he or she is led to believe that they are loved, abuse becomes their language of love. By contrast, if patience and care is the language then that is how they learn to express themselves.

I have always taught my boys that they have the potential to make a difference. Rather than just being part of a crowd, they are important and have something to offer just like everyone else does. This enhanced their self-esteem and gave them a sense of worth and responsibility. I spent a lot of time explaining to my boys how the world works. I wanted them to understand and appreciate their surroundings. I would tell them to be good to their teachers because he or she was a person like me who gets up every morning and goes to work, and they wouldn't like it if someone was naughty or mean to me.

My boys often laugh at how, by explaining everything and opening their eyes to the world, I robbed them of their innocence. They say they couldn't be ratbags like every other kid in school 'because we understood too much'.

I certainly had a lot of theories on parenting in the early years. I strongly believed that my role as a mother was to nurture and protect and build the foundation of a loving, capable adult with self-esteem. In particular, an adult who, upon closing their eyes at night, feels a sense of peace and stability within themselves. The world would teach them the rest.

I was fortunate that while my sons were growing up they were surrounded by family and friends. I continued the usual practice of hosting Christmas, Easter and birthdays at my house. We played music and everyone would dance. Needless to say, there was always plenty of food. I would cook for an army, always ensuring that I made my sons' favourite dishes. I had learned a lot about hosting parties by observing my parents as a child, and I think I had it down pat: lots of noise, people, food and laughter. I always tried to make birthdays special for the boys by decorating the house with balloons and streamers, and baking big birthday cakes. I would often hire a large inflatable jumping castle that would be set up in the backyard for all the children to play on.

My father would usually come over and cook when we were celebrating. One year he taught the boys how to marinade olives. He bought a large box of green olives from the market and spent a whole day showing them how to split the olives one by one with a cleaver and then soak them in salty water for two days. He then returned to show them how to dress them with oil, chilli and garlic.

I got through my law degree by studying a few subjects over summer school, often bringing Christos to uni. I would place him on the floor next to me in class with pencils and colouring books to keep him busy for the hour or two. He would crawl between the students' legs and rattle his pencil tin to make noise. He loved it when it was time to go home as I routinely bought him a chocolate from the vending machine in the foyer, which made him feel special, as though I were rewarding him for keeping me company for the day. I had finished my studies before Myles was born.

In 1997 I was thrilled to be admitted to practice. It had been a long road with a lot of distractions but I always knew I'd get there. I had set out on this journey many years ago and had finally achieved success. As a girl, I had assumed that success is not possible without an education. But I was beginning to understand that the integrity of the person is what drives success, rather than a university degree. By the time I was admitted, I had already achieved a lot. I had remained focused and driven and was never daunted by hard work. I had been fearless in setting goals and single-minded in accomplishing them.

Admission into practice was a great achievement, but I had earned it. I knew I didn't want to work as a solicitor and set my sights on becoming a barrister. But there was no rush. I was well aware that as soon as I signed the bar roll, I'd have to work full-time. For now I wanted to spend time with the boys.

In 1998 I took the year off to stay at home with Myles and Christos. I really hadn't had much of an opportunity to enjoy being a mother without other factors competing for my attention. I had also been feeling run-down and had become unwell in late 1997. As it turned out, I had glandular fever so I definitely needed to rest.

We were still living in the old house in Brighton, tossing up whether to renovate or rebuild. Eventually we decided to bulldoze the old house and build two new homes on the land. Although the block wasn't that wide it was deep, with enough room for two townhouses. I had never built a house before, but I found a great architect and builder who understood my vision and I was confident they would deliver. I wanted my children to grow up in a comfortable house that they loved.

By 2000 our property development was complete. We would move in to one townhouse and the other would serve as an investment property. We had done well and I was keen to keep growing our property portfolio.

In late 2001 we bought another property, also in Brighton, close to the boys' school. We subdivided that property and built two large townhouses complete with sandstone driveways, seventeen-foot ceilings, wrought-iron fences and a large entertaining area that opened onto a pool. That development took a bit longer due to unexpected delays, so we lived in our first development until 2004.

I constantly had a project on the go. Apart from law, property development became my new passion. I knew that soon I'd be able to buy a house in the street where I grew up, on the beach; it was only a matter of time before one came on the market.

My husband and I seemed to have overcome our tumultuous relationship history. We were enjoying parenthood and the future looked promising. We were both in well-paid jobs and we had income from our properties. We were getting along pretty well, both on the same path and sharing a vision for the future. We never spent a day apart and would always travel together on business trips overseas and interstate, taking our boys with us when we could. We had come a long way from the first house in which we'd lived when I was a student and he was unemployed. We had a similar sense of humour and could talk for hours.

I still knew that I couldn't rely on him entirely. I was well aware that if I was ever needy, he could become cold and argumentative. I knew the deal and worked tirelessly to make sure I never had to depend on him. I just accepted that people are people; they are who they are.

But it's an inescapable fact of life that all of us, at some point, experience times of vulnerability and need. During those times, we should be able to go home, close the door, and find comfort and support in our partner. It's the basic rule of friendship.

CHAPTER FIVE

Life at the Bar
(1999–2015)

I N 1999 MYLES started three-year-old kinder at Brighton Grammar where Christos was a student in Grade Five. It was perfect timing for me to join the bar and I started the bar readers' course—which is necessary before one can become a member of the Victorian Bar—in March of that year.

We were required to hand in written work, prepare cases and run moot or mock court cases. We were filmed conducting every case and then assessed and critiqued by a judge from either the county or supreme court. Sitting in a small room, we'd watch a re-run of our performance and anxiously wait for the judge's feedback. We were taught simple things like don't click your pen, it's distracting; don't say 'Your Honour' over and over, and don't look down when you're talking as it obstructs your words. We were taught how to run a case, how to prepare opening and closing submissions, how to lead evidence, cross-examine and re-examine, and how to enter a plea if our client was pleading guilty and was to be sentenced. We were all aware of the responsibility we were assuming; our client's future was often in our hands. I knew I would be representing clients who were facing time in jail, who risked losing their children in custody disputes and were possibly about to lose their home. The scenarios were endless. Each day I was in court I would be representing someone who was stressed, worried and anxious about their future. I had to know exactly what I was doing and be adequately prepared, because failing to prepare was preparing to fail.

Several judges reviewed my performances. I'd already met some of them at bar dinners I'd attended while at uni. I was particularly fond of Judge Frank Walsh. He was a county court judge who contracted polio as a child and consequently walked with a walking stick. He reminded me of the boy in the children's book *I Can Jump Puddles*. Written by Alan Marshall in 1955, the book recounts the author's childhood having contracted polio when he was six years old. I met Alan at school when he visited the Grade

Five students. He told us about his meeting with the Queen of England and how nervous he was when he had to speak before an audience. He managed to overcome his nerves by reminding himself that they were all just people, like himself, who would get up in the morning, brush their teeth and get dressed. His advice on public speaking has stayed with me. Alan's struggle taught him many valuable life lessons, not least humility.

Judge Walsh also seemed to understand the value of humility and compassion for the human condition. At his retirement ceremony in 2003, he delivered a moving speech that described a trip with his wife to Hanging Rock soon after they met. Despite his disability, she invited him to climb to the top of the mountain. When he reached the summit he was exhausted and laughing, he said that he 'fell in love on top of the mountain' and that he has 'continued to laugh with [his] wife for forty years'. Reaching his retirement, Judge Walsh proclaimed, 'We are still at the top of the mountain and now I propose to spend the balance of my life ever so gently descending the mountain with Mary.'

As well as acknowledging his wife, Walsh paid tribute to women in law. He said there had been a 'gradual redress for the errors and injustices of history now that women had taken their rightful place at the bar, on the bench and on juries'. He went on to say: 'My judicial career has enabled me to understand that all people are to be accorded the dignity which is their right and heritage as human beings.' Judge Walsh was praised by his colleagues for bringing his deep humanity and his comprehension of people's hopes, expectations and faults to his court.

Until I attended his retirement ceremony I didn't really know a lot about him. I had never appeared before his court but I knew he was a good man. I was always moved by his ability to say so much in a few words. He could encapsulate the essence of an entire scenario in one line. Like many barristers and judges, he was a wordsmith and was articulate and eloquent.

Judge Walsh was one of my mentors and I felt privileged to be taught by him. One day, after critiquing one of my filmed performances in court, he quite unexpectedly said, 'Gina, don't ever lose your femininity. When you walk into a courtroom you will be a breath of fresh air.'

It was exactly what I needed to hear at that time and I thanked him for his encouragement. I hadn't ever discussed my appearance with Judge Walsh, but somehow he'd sensed that my flamboyant style was on my mind as I was about to enter the boys' club at the bar. Perhaps he'd seen women compromise their femininity in the past; regardless, all I know is that those few words of affirmation were all I needed to remain comfortable being me.

Throughout my legal career, I have maintained my sense of personal style and always dressed up. I could never have relinquished my love for fashion, particularly as it defined my formative years. Once I started at the bar, I tried to dress relatively conservatively, but always with an individual twist that would change according to the fashion—be it colour, style, shoes, shoulder pads, lace skirts or peplum jackets. I still had big hair, a throwback to the eighties, and yes, it's still big today. I love to look glamorous, and don't know how to dress in a dowdy or masculine style.

I noticed that many of the women at the bar tried to blend into the male culture by becoming more masculine; their voices became deeper and their hair got shorter. Perhaps it was easier that way; perhaps it gave them more credibility. Only a few women dressed up, but the majority didn't. I saw hairy legs crammed into sheer skin-toned hosiery. Perish the thought; I wouldn't be seen dead like that. In fact, I would make sure my legs were shaved and body bronze applied *even if* I were dead.

During my years at uni, there weren't many girls studying law, and only five completed the bar readers' course compared to forty-six men. If I think back to school, most of the girls who became lawyers and doctors were bookworms and tended to be on the quiet and conservative side. They certainly weren't women who'd run fashion stores in the eighties and nineties, the most flamboyant era in fashion history. So it was unlikely that I was going to come across someone like me. Yes, I was a bit over the top. But after all, I had been a girl for longer than I had been a lawyer, so losing my femininity in order to fit in was never an option.

I was only ever given the boys' club routine twice in my career. On one occasion, very early in my practice, I was opposed to an aggressive barrister who thought that I should type the orders we had settled in court. When I asked him why, he explained that he wasn't very good at typing. 'Well,' I told him, 'neither am I.' Apart from which, they were his clients' terms and therefore his responsibility.

The second time I was made to feel like I'd trespassed into the boys' club was several years later at the family court. A senior member of counsel asked me if I was a social worker. I explained that I was the barrister acting for the opposing party. I asked him his name and he refused, suggesting that if I really was a barrister I should know him. I explained that I didn't know who he was, that we hadn't met, and that I was going to get a coffee to give him time to get over himself. I've never had a problem since.

*

I SIGNED THE bar roll on 29 May 1999 using a new Mont Blanc pen, a gift from a colleague to acknowledge my admission.

I was thirty-three years old. After years of focus, determination and endless distractions, finally I had arrived. The day was marked by a ceremony, lots of photos and a function in the evening. It felt a bit like a wedding; it certainly was an occasion signifying a commitment. This was a plan for life and I felt more conscientious about the job than ambitious.

My family was really happy for me. Mum gave me a ten-carat amethyst and two diamonds to have set in a gold ring that was made up a few months later. My father congratulated me over the phone, saying, 'I'm-a so proud of you!' My sisters were relieved that I had achieved my life-plan and my brothers were impressed that I had persevered and attained my goal. Many friends and family members called to wish me well and congratulate me.

But the day was not without its stress. My husband joined me for lunch and to share in the celebrations. Upon entering my chambers he noticed a gift and card from a male colleague, a barrister with whom I'd been friends since uni. We'd had a brief romance during one of the many periods of separation before we were married. It was a long time ago, we were now friends and he was certainly no threat to the marriage, which my husband knew. Regardless, he was upset about the gift and already feeling threatened that I was working in a predominantly male profession. He hadn't said as much, but I knew because he'd get jealous whenever

Above: My mother and grandmother at my first wedding. Hali is on my mother's knee.

Right: Dancing with Teresa and Rosie, and Christos is in my arms.

Below: Christos in 1991 when we took him to the go-carts and he couldn't contain his excitement.

Right: My second wedding day, this time in a garden with a celebrant.

Below: All the family at Myles's christening in 1997.

Bottom right: Christos and Myles in 1997.

Left: Myles' birthday a few months before I was diagnosed with cancer.

Below: Christos with BooBoo and Pepsi in 2003 after I came home from hospital.

Bottom left: Christos and Myles in 2000.

Right right: Christos and Myles with me in Venice in 2004.

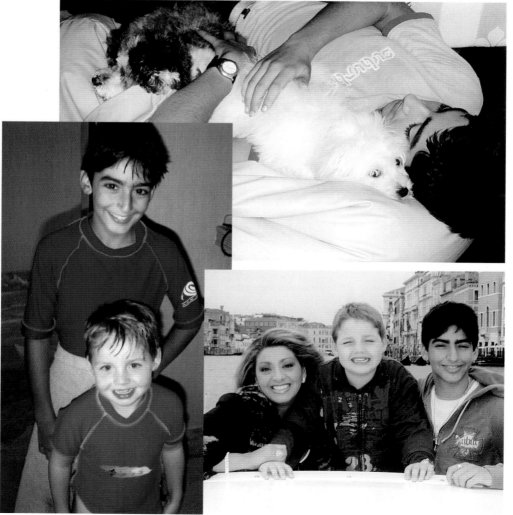

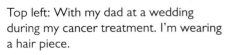

Top left: With my dad at a wedding during my cancer treatment. I'm wearing a hair piece.

Above right: Robed and wigged in front of the Supreme Court in 2013.

Above left: With Myles on his seventeenth birthday in 2013.

Right: Me and Christos at a Foxtel event in 2013.

Top left: Behind the scenes for a newspaper photoshoot in 2014. It was the first time the boys had been interviewed with me.

Above: Me and my mum on Christmas Day in 2014.

Left: At my Gina Liano shoe launch with my partner's mother and beautiful daughter. Both came to hear my speech at my old school, Star of the Sea.

Top left: Foxtel's poster for season one of Real Housewives of Melbourne.

Top right: In the blue dress I wore in the opening of season one.

Left: Foxtel's poster for the second series of Real Housewives of Melbourne with two new cast members.

Above: The cast attending the TV week Logie awards in 2014.

Top left: Attending Fashion Aid where I donated for auction the blue dress I wore in the opening of Real Housewives of Melbourne.

Top right: As an ambassador for the Cancer Council of Victoria at the Caulfield Races family day.

Centre left: Behind the scenes in season two during filming of the master interviews.

Above: Hair and, of course, makeup.

Left: The Gina Liano crystal shoe launch that was filmed in season two.

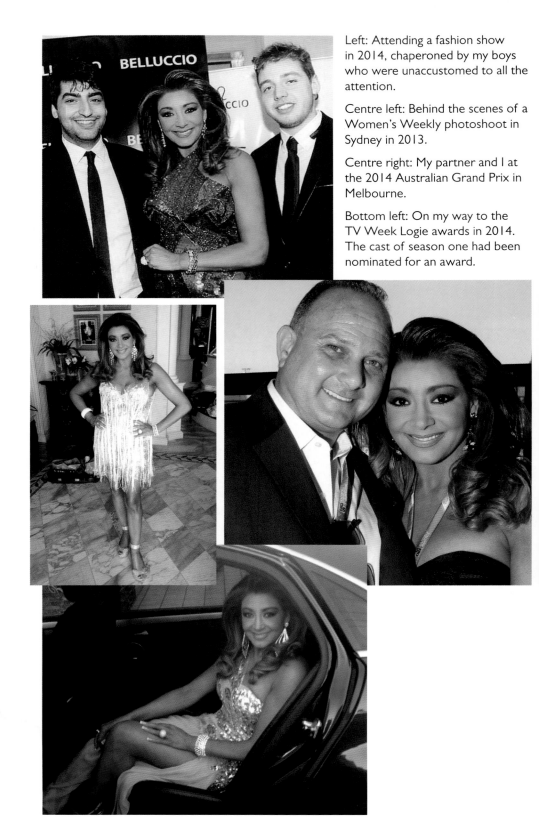

Left: Attending a fashion show in 2014, chaperoned by my boys who were unaccustomed to all the attention.

Centre left: Behind the scenes of a Women's Weekly photoshoot in Sydney in 2013.

Centre right: My partner and I at the 2014 Australian Grand Prix in Melbourne.

Bottom left: On my way to the TV Week Logie awards in 2014. The cast of season one had been nominated for an award.

he saw me speaking to a man. I suppose those years of separation and reconciliation created some insecurity, but it was no excuse for being cruel.

As I was putting on my robe to get ready for the ceremony, my husband said, 'I think we should end the marriage.'

'Are you serious?' I said. I couldn't believe what he was saying. He was obviously trying to upset me and it was working.

I told him to get out. He left and didn't look back. I was furious that he was trying to ruin my day. I felt that I could never forgive him and didn't care if I never saw him again. He was well aware of how hard I'd worked; he'd watched me study all night, work all day and sit my exams. He'd come to my graduation and to my admission to practice. I had shared so much with him. But he didn't seem to care. All that mattered to him was that I had received a gift from someone he didn't like and he was jealous.

I arrived home late that night, dreading having to look at him. He greeted me at the door, asking where I had been and why I was so late. He started to argue with me, accusing me of smelling like men's aftershave.

Dear Lord, was he serious? He knew full well where I had been. Instead of focusing on my achievement, all he could do was question my integrity. I said that the smell must be his own aftershave wafting up in the humidity of his body that had become overheated with insane jealousy. This was far from good; I was about to embark on my career and he was already giving me grief. We had not separated since we were married, but I knew the signs and I could feel the relationship falling apart.

We argued for several days, and my sense of happiness about achieving a significant milestone became submerged in the misery of our arguments. Two weeks later I'd had enough. I was full of resentment, and I knew that it would be difficult to recover. I decided that I had no choice but to end the relationship. I asked him to leave and he moved out a few days later.

I was really annoyed to be on my own again, and facing life as a single mother. But I knew this scenario was far preferable to raising Myles and Christos in an environment of arguments and bitterness. I wanted to enjoy my career without having to put up with a jealous, threatened husband lurking in the background.

Despite my husband's absence, I maintained my daily routine and was managing fine. I was upset but I remained focused. I took the boys to school every morning and picked them up after work. I cooked a meal every night and placed a large clay pot at the head of the table where my husband had usually sat for dinner. I felt that the pot was filling the void. I know this might seem mean and it's obviously not true but I was really annoyed with him. I was so relieved that I had chosen a career that could sustain my children, and that I wasn't locked into an unhappy marriage due to financial dependence. My boys were okay. It wasn't the ideal situation but we were always happy to be together.

I can't recall the exact circumstances—there had been so many break-ups and reconciliations over the years—but we got back together months later. Despite my resentment, I admit that I did miss him. He was a great father and I obviously still loved him and thought there was hope for our marriage. I put our separation behind us and focused on the future.

That summer I worked over the Christmas break and was briefed in an urgent application before the children's court in a child abuse case. Most of the barristers in that jurisdiction were on summer vacation so weren't available. I was briefed to prosecute. I had never worked with children and found the jurisdiction confronting and difficult. The substance of the case was distressing. The paramount consideration was the safety of the child, and I needed to ensure that the child was not exposed to an unacceptable risk of harm.

The case ran for three days, and I somehow managed to avoid bursting into tears. I was exhausted by the end of it, but relieved that the child was safe. I was unaware of it at the time—I felt like I never wanted to work in the children's court again—but this case signified the start of my career in prosecuting child abuse cases. Since then, I have run hundreds of cases. All of them are deeply distressing, although some more than others. Many cases I can relate to as a mother and as an adolescent on a difficult journey. I have clear memories of how I felt at different stages of my life, and can see and feel the heart of the child in every case.

I'm often asked how I manage to go home at night and switch off from the emotional turmoil of the day. It's a good question. Sometimes it's really difficult, especially when you've heard a child crying in court—for example, because their drug-addicted mother can no longer care for them and they have to live with a relative until she recovers; or their mother is the victim of domestic violence and is struggling to break away from an abusive relationship. No child wants to be separated from his or her parent. Some children react worse than others. I have always worked hard to put supports in place so parent and child can be reconciled. I know what it feels like not to have your mum around.

I do try and force myself to forget some of the more distressing situations I encounter. Over the years I have developed a way of coping by not paying attention to names. By forgetting names, the facts of the various cases all mesh together into themes rather than remain as personal, individualised events.

This coping strategy has caused an unexpected occupational hazard: my name amnesia is not confined to court and I find myself forgetting many people's names, even in social situations. When someone tells me his or her name I generally hear a sound rather than a name. So that's why I may appear at times to be 'on vagation'.

I didn't embark on my career with a clear view of the area of law I wanted to practise. I was drawn to criminal law and hoped to work in either defence or prosecution. The first case I ever ran was in the family court where breakups and custody are the order of the day. It was a fairly simple case and my client didn't need to be there. At first I found the language and process of the court confusing but I watched the other barristers and quickly worked things out. It was a steep and rapid learning curve. I also appeared in many civil cases and realised that I prefer to work with matters of the heart rather than the wallet.

I have seen a lot of disturbing cases over the years, and my experiences have shifted my perspective on things. Trivial matters that others might become fixated on rarely affect me. I've learned to brush a lot of things off knowing there's so much more to this world.

My children feel a sense of personal safety knowing that I work to protect children. I think they feel confident that I will always look out for their best interests, and I always have.

In those early years I rarely took time off work, apart from when I was travelling overseas. I would work through every summer break when most barristers take leave, and kept consolidating my practice. I also maintained my hand in property development. It was on a small scale but we had done well and I wanted to keep growing our property port-folio. I was no stranger to hard work and was accustomed to putting in a lot of effort. I certainly didn't expect to be given anything without commitment and dedication. I would work for long hours, often through the night, to prepare cases. I would get up early in the morning, get my boys ready for school and go to court. Some days were mentally and physically draining and I would arrive home from work and collapse on the couch.

By 2002 I had run hundreds of cases and was feeling very tired. Each morning I'd wake up more exhausted than when I went to sleep. I felt like I really needed a rest; years of hard work had begun to take their toll. My husband was planning a business trip overseas later that year so I decided to accompany him and take a well-deserved break. Simply knowing there was a holiday on the horizon gave me a burst of energy. We had travelled to Europe in 2000 and had a wonderful time. It had been my first visit to Italy and I immediately felt at home. In Florence there were women everywhere who looked like me. I visited family whom I hadn't seen since I was a child and connected with them as though I'd seen them yesterday. I loved every minute of it. I returned home with an extra suitcase of clothing, shoes and handbags. It had only been two years since that trip but it felt like a lifetime had passed.

This time we planned to be away during our winter, and therefore summer in Europe. I love summer and was looking forward to the warm weather and sleeping in. On our itinerary were visits to Rome, Florence, Venice, London, Scotland and the USA. I couldn't wait. Myles and Christos went to stay with Myles's grandmother in Tasmania, and we were off.

Unfortunately, for much of our holiday I felt quite unwell. I had a couple of strange episodes in London and Italy that were a bit worrying. Upon our return home I still wasn't feeling great. I had night sweats and was really tired. I put it down to a lifetime of effort and that I had hit a wall. I had felt this way a few years before and had spent a few weeks in hospital with glandular fever. I hoped I wasn't having a relapse. I pushed through, returned to work and started running back-to-back trials, but was looking forward to the Christmas break. I felt like I needed some time off to rest.

As usual, I hosted Christmas for my family at my house, with friends also dropping in. I put on a big spread, still inspired by Christmases of my childhood, and prepared lasagna, schnitzels, roast, salads, antipasto, cheese platters with grapes and strawberries with homemade desserts such as tiramisu, cheesecake and pavlova. I loved celebrating with my family and was enjoying my new house. As per usual, there was music playing and lots of laughter, noise and dancing. Dancing had become a family tradition that each of us had passed on to our children. When Christos was growing up he would come into the shop and dance in front of the mirror to Earth, Wind and Fire and Michael Jackson.

The Christmas break revived me and I was feeling better. I returned to work in January 2003 and was planning another overseas trip in early February, this time to Hong Kong for Chinese New Year. I was getting along well with my husband, the boys were happy, I was excited about our new house and my practice at the bar was booming. The future looked bright and full of promise.

CHAPTER SIX

Determined to Survive (2003–2008)

IN 1997 WHEN I was thirty, I spent time in hospital recovering from glandular fever as I mentioned previously. I already had two children; had married twice; attained three university degrees; bought, developed and sold properties; had a string of clothing stores and was working as a lawyer. It was clear that I didn't have a stop button. I would work all day, study all night and survived on about three hours' sleep for many years. What was I thinking? Who does all that? So it's no surprise I ended up really run-down. Crash and burn is what they call it.

Looking back, I realise that the mindset responsible for my demise was inherited from a long line of women in my family who were high achievers and hard workers. I believed that what I was doing was normal. However, my body obviously didn't agree and was finally forcing me to stop. I spent about three months in bed. I had weakness, lethargy, migraines, difficulty breathing, and a constant pain in my left ribcage that X-rays revealed to be due to four broken ribs. I hadn't experienced a trauma so the cause remained a mystery. The doctors described it as a 'spontaneous fracture'. Evidently, I had crashed, burned and burst at the seams.

I struggled pretty badly with this illness. At times it actually felt terminal; I was in a lot pain so I spent countless days in and out of hospital, sometimes being transported by ambulance. I knew that I had been working too hard but my malaise felt deeper than that. I was carrying a lot of hurt and frustration and it felt like it was now manifesting as a physical illness.

Although I'm not a practising Catholic, I believe that we operate on three levels: body, soul and spirit. I felt that my soul was eternal, as do all Christians, but my body was struggling and my spirit felt broken. Which meant that I was operating on two out of three cylinders and I needed help.

I felt that I was in a crisis, so I did what many people do in such a situation: I started searching for answers. I looked for spiritual explanations, seeking guidance from spiritual healers, psychics and Eastern and Western religions. I discovered that my Catholic education had only taught me the practice of Christianity—in other words, how to live as a Christian by following the ten commandments, for instance. But I hadn't understood that the purpose of religion is faith—a belief that I am not alone, that there is a larger force who will look after me, and that I could hand over all my hurt and frustration to that force and be relieved of the burden that was making me ill. I strongly believed that there was a metaphysical dimension to my illness.

I learned that most religions believe in a god that 'created' them, and that prayer is the way to communicate with that god. Indeed, this seems to be a universal belief, and all over the world there are monuments and temples built in honour of faith. Faith simply means belief. I obviously can't prove there is a God so at best I can only believe there is one. When I look at my children, I can't believe that they are simply an accident of nature; surely they were created by a divine force?

The problem with glandular fever is that pathology sometimes only picks it up after you've had the illness, so when I was in the midst of all this suffering I had no idea what was ailing me. Back then, I left the hospital and decided I needed to get away to try to recover and convalesce. My cousin Rosie invited me to the coast to stay with her at her yoga teacher's home, where she was house-sitting at the time.

Rosie, who lived with us when we were growing up, was like my little sister. She had been studying healing massage and yoga. She and Teresa had already started considering their spirituality and were searching for direction, attending yoga retreats and visiting the 'holy mother', an Indian guru who allegedly possessed healing powers.

Rosie picked me up from home as I wasn't well enough to drive. We arrived at the house late at night, I noticed that the walls were lined with photos of gurus and Eastern symbols of wellness. I felt that I had come to the right place. We had something to eat and I crawled into bed. Although I was relieved to be away, I was torn with the guilt of having left my boys behind. Myles was twelve months old and Christos was seven. I felt guilty that they needed me yet I wasn't well enough to look after them. I couldn't understand why I was feeling so unwell. My left side felt pierced and I couldn't shake the pain. I lay in bed thinking, How did I end up in this situation? I had a child and a baby, a career and responsibilities, yet I was bedridden.

I started questioning God; had I done something wrong? I had all the motivation in the world, but my body would not let me move. I started demanding answers from God. I'd had enough of this. I needed to get up and live the life I had always planned and worked so hard to establish. I lay in bed tossing and turning. I couldn't sleep, the pain in my side was too severe and I felt anxious and restless. I had always believed in God, but I had never called out to him before.

Suddenly, I heard a voice. It was a voice in my head but it was audible and clear. It said, 'John 19:36.' I stopped whinge-ing and asked, 'What?' Then again, I heard it: 'John 19:36.' I looked around the room. 'God, is that you?' I whispered in disbelief. I thought I had lost my mind. Finally, I said, 'Okay, so God if it is you, I'm going to forget this ever hap-pened, and if you really want to talk to me, then let's speak in the morning.'

When I was a child, my grandmother had told me stories about God communicating with people. But I never believed her and put it down to her being superstitious and dramatic. I wasn't like her; I was an educated woman with an analytical mind and this just did not compute, so I tried to ignore it.

I can't remember falling asleep but I was woken early in the morning with that same voice: 'John 19:36', over and over again. It was driving me mad. I had to get up and investigate what this was about. I didn't like my chances of finding a bible in the house of a Buddhist yoga instructor, but nevertheless I started searching. It felt quite urgent, like the feeling you get when you need to make a phone call three minutes before the close of business. I went through every bookshelf in the house. My cousin was still sleeping, and I wanted to find the answer before she woke up. I didn't want her to think I had lost my mind.

Just as I was about to give up, I opened my suitcase and a bible fell out of the top pocket. I couldn't believe it. It had been given to Myles by his godmother at his christening a few months earlier. I don't know how or why it was in the suitcase but it was. I was starting to feel very confused about all of this, and my logical legal mind was challenged.

I opened the bible and, to my surprise, discovered that there is indeed a chapter 19 in the book of John and a verse 36. But the real surprise was the chapter's title: 'Jesus's side was pierced'—the same words I'd been uttering that night, asking God, 'Why does my side feel pierced?'

What did this mean? It was all so cryptic, but I knew it signified something. I just wasn't sure what.

Rosie woke up and came into the kitchen where I was standing at the benchtop, looking deeply perplexed, the open bible in front of me. She asked me what was wrong. I told her what had happened during the night, and what I'd just read in the bible. She was equally confused, but then she started crying. She knew it meant something. How could this be a coincidence? She had been worried about me for weeks.

Later that day my husband arrived with Myles. I told him what had happened, and he was similarly mystified. On the way home, a colleague rang to ask how I was, and to invite me to attend a healing service at the local church. I hadn't told him about the incident with the bible, nor had I ever discussed religion with this guy, so this was a very strange coincidence. I hadn't been to church—apart from weddings, christenings and funerals—since I'd left school. Too many coincidences. Too many signs. It was all very confusing.

I felt compelled to attend the healing service and agreed to meet my friend at the church in a couple of hours, which was not going to be easy. Apart from being unwell, I was two hours away, it was raining heavily and my husband had suddenly come down with a fever and couldn't come with me or look after Myles. How was I going to defy these odds? I was used to flying in the face of challenges, so even though I hadn't been out of bed for over three months I was determined to get to the church. If God had spoken to me in a house full of gurus, he might have a lot to say in his own house.

By the time we got home my husband was feeling even worse. It was a Sunday evening and Christos was still at his father's. Determined to get to this healing service, I put Myles in the car and left him in the care of a friend. As I drove to the church, which was far from my home, I started to worry that I wasn't well enough to make it there or to get home afterwards. I didn't want to burden anyone with my illness.

I did make it, however, and walked into the church, albeit a bit late. People were singing, it was very loud, and suddenly

I began to feel weird. Where on earth was I? I started to perspire, my pulse started to race, I had sweaty palms, was dizzy, my head was hurting, I needed to sit down. What had I done? I needed to get out of there, I was about to faint. The loud music was like a torture.

I didn't feel well enough to leave so I sat there thinking, 'Please God, get them to shut up.' And just like that, coincidently, the singing stopped. Thank God!

As soon as the singing ceased my headache subsided, the pain in my side went away, my pulse settled down and I felt heat radiating throughout my body. Now, I am as much of a sceptic as the next person, but what happened then defied logic. As the music stopped, I felt my illness lift. I turned to my colleague and said, 'What's going on here?' He looked at me and smiled. He'd attended healing services before and had witnessed people being healed. He'd been watching me struggle and could see that something had happened. I sat there, even more confused. Who was I? Why should I be healed? Could this be real?

I walked out of that church feeling transformed. I couldn't believe what had happened to me. Why was I crying? I never cry. How had the pain in my side gone away? How had an enormous ulcer in my mouth disappeared? This was amazing. Why had I never heard about this? I felt like God had come and pulled me out of a black hole.

Now what? What was next? How could I explain this to my husband and my family? He was surely going to think I had gone mad. I drove home, picking up my son on the way. When I arrived home my husband was feeling better. I told him what had happened. He was as baffled as I was, but he could notice a change in me. I showed him that the ulcer in my mouth had gone.

I now had the feeling that things were going to be different. How could I ignore what had happened? I simply couldn't. I knew that I was about to embark on a new journey. People can talk you into and out of philosophies but they cannot talk you out of an experience. No-one can take that away from you, or convince you otherwise if it happened.

Obviously I knew this whole God thing didn't start with me; it had been going on since the beginning of time so there was clearly something in it. I could not accept what had happened simply on face value. I needed to investigate so I started studying theology. You won't ever hear me preach about what I believe. I respect that everyone is on their own journey, and each one of us believes in what feels right.

I learned many things through my studies, but my over-riding lesson was that God works in mysterious ways, and his timing is perfect. I also know that we live in a physical world and while I felt protected and safe, things are still going to happen that aren't related to God.

*

IN MARCH 2003 I was diagnosed with cancer. I was thirty-six years old and had been feeling ill for about eight months. In August the previous year, while on holiday with my husband, I was shopping at Harrods in London when I suddenly felt very unwell. I went back to the hotel and lay down. I started getting shivers and my jaw was chattering. That night I had night sweats so I guessed I was coming down with something, but that I'd be okay.

Our next stop was Italy. Anyone who's been to Rome in August knows that it can be unbearably hot. But I generally enjoy the heat, and I was excited to be in Rome. We walked around for hours looking at ancient relics, taking photos and eating ice-cream. I had forgotten about my strange turn in London and felt okay, but the night sweats continued. I complained to the hotel about the air-conditioning and wondered whether I had eaten something that had gone off. Italians have a habit of leaving food out in the open and eating it when it's on the turn as the bacteria tastes delicious, giving the food a full, ripe flavour. I wasn't about to let my discomfort spoil our trip so I soldiered on.

One hot night in Rome, I experienced the same shivers I'd had in London, but this time there was no excuse for feeling chilled to the bone: it was about forty degrees Celsius.

I couldn't shake the chills so sat next to an open flame wood-fired oven while we ate dinner. My husband was perspiring but I was still cold. It was clear that I had to investigate this when I got home. Was I having hormonal changes? I was thirty-five, there was no reason to feel like this.

A few weeks later we returned home and I went to the doctor, wondering whether perhaps I'd drunk some bad water during our travels. I consulted one specialist after another. Each doctor was concerned because the glands were up under my arms. I had endless blood tests and scans, including a gallium scan, to check if I had leukemia. All the tests were clear.

I ended up seeing an endocrinologist, thinking the night sweats must be hormonal. She checked my thyroid and found a tumour on my parathyroid, but as far as she could tell, it was benign. She diagnosed me with hyperparathyroidism, elevated calcium and low vitamin D. She didn't think it necessary to have an urgent operation. She suggested I take vitamin supplements, and she warned me to expect the symptoms to be non-specific, such as aches, pains, moans and groans. I thought, okay, I can live with that until I get a break to book in for surgery.

About a month later I was at work running a trial. As I walked into court I drew a blank. I could not remember the name of the case as I stood up to announce my appearance to the judge. Clearly something was very wrong. I walked out of the court into the practitioner's room and bang—I felt something pop in my head. Then I saw stars, like I was about to faint, and my body was gripped by cold shivers. I immediately went down to sickbay and called my husband to come and pick me up. I then called the endocrinologist and described what had happened. She said that my experience was not consistent with hyperparathyroidism.

Concerned, I spent the week consulting doctors and specialists. All the tests were clear. No-one could explain what had happened; nothing untoward was revealed. So I went back to work and put the experience down to working too hard and being a bit run-down.

Christmas and New Year passed without incident. In early 2003, my husband and I were travelling in Hong Kong when I started to feel very unwell again: the night sweats were back. Something was clearly wrong; this had been going on for too long. The SARS virus was rampaging throughout Asia at the time and I hoped I hadn't caught it.

When I got home, still feeling really unwell, I went to see the doctor again. He referred me to a specialist who booked me in for a day procedure to explore what was going on. And bingo … there it was: bowel cancer.

Upon hearing the diagnosis, I was immediately defensive. No-one in my family had ever had cancer! I looked at my husband, whose eyes had become bright red. Not like he was emotional or about to cry, but as if a bus had just hit him. I turned back to the doctor and said, 'I don't think so … let me tell you, this body is not playing host to that invasion. Get it out, get it out today.'

Needless to say, it doesn't work like that. A surgeon needs to be booked along with a hospital theatre and nurses. It wasn't a triage situation where I was in the emergency room. I was going to have to wait.

We got in the car, both of us gobsmacked. I was hoping my husband would be able to cope with the situation and not become cold and distant as he tended to do when I was unwell. It had been a long-term concern of mine that my marriage would not endure if I ever became seriously ill, but I put this worry aside for now; it was the least of my concerns.

I rang Mum. I started off saying, 'Don't be worried …' and then I told her I had cancer. As eloquent as I usually am, it was the hardest sentence I've ever had to string together.

Mum hung up the phone and burst into tears. She was at work—she was now a practising psychologist—it was just before midday on a Monday morning and there were patients in the waiting room. She ran into her colleague's room who was a doctor. He had to sedate her. Once she'd calmed down and composed herself, he drove her to my house.

I don't remember calling Teresa, but somehow she turned up. I know I must have called Ben too, but it's all a blur. I do remember some of the other calls I made. The reaction of people who love you when you tell them devastating news is quite humbling; it gave me an inkling of what was to come.

Needless to say, the journey through cancer is as traumatic for family and friends as it is for the person who is ill. They can't help but imagine life without you as they evaluate the implications of this news and consider the worst-possible consequences. One of my aunties burst into tears on the phone. She was wailing, as Italians do, and asked me to promise her that I wouldn't die. 'Promise me you will live and become a judge one day!' she cried.

Another family member became so bewildered by what I was telling her that through her tears she cried, 'What's cancer?'

The most interesting reaction came from Bettina. When I told her she said, 'Of course you do. Don't you know that one in three people get cancer? … I'm never going to get through this fitting.'

Anybody who knows Bettina is aware that she's a tough cookie. She's worked hard and is best described as 'a gun'. Nevertheless, her reaction was unexpected and tough. She was furious and annoyed; she didn't want me to be sick. She didn't want to hear what I was telling her. Obviously, she was in shock and didn't know how to react. As tough as she is, she walked out of that fitting, sat down in the corridor and cried.

The sad reality is that Bettina's statistics were generous. These days, two out of three people get cancer. I have been told that fifty women a day in Australia are diagnosed with breast or gynecological cancers. I know that every single one of those girls have experienced something like I have. I call them girls because when it comes to fear, there's no such thing as being a grown-up.

The front doorbell rang all afternoon as one relative after another turned up, each trying their best to look composed, but each failing to hold it together. Christos was home from school that day as he was unwell. He came downstairs to a living-room full of people crying. He was twelve years old, mature enough to understand that something serious was going on.

Immediately I realised that the situation had to be managed—and fast. I needed everyone to believe that I was going to be alright. I recognised the fear in their eyes; I had the same fear in me. But I didn't want my family and friends to feel afraid. I wanted them to be strong for me. How could I rely on them to fight for me if I started losing the battle? They needed to be courageous. I thought to myself, God, I need your help. What am I going to do?

The nuns at school had taught me that faith is the opposite of fear. I thought that if I pray and my family witnesses my faith, they may gain some comfort in that. My past experiences had strengthened my faith, which was just as well as I knew I would need a lot of faith to get through this challenge. I needed to be fearless.

I sat down with my family and asked them to join hands. It didn't matter if they shared my faith or not; this was a crisis and I was calling in the big guns. I suggested that everyone close their eyes while I prayed out loud. I prayed for about ten minutes as I had a long list of things to say. I asked God for his help. I thanked Him for bringing everyone to be with me and asked Him to give us all strength and courage. I reminded Him that I had been healed in the past and this time I was putting myself at the foot of the cross and 'I wasn't moving'. There wasn't a dry eye in the room.

Poor little Christos; he needed counselling after such a display. Over the next few months while I was undergoing surgery and treatment, I was told he'd often go missing from school for hours. No-one could find him after school and he was often absent from class. He'd always turn up just before it got to the critical point of calling the police. Myles eventually told me that his brother was in the school chapel and would sit in there for hours. I guess when I put myself at the foot of the cross, Christos followed.

That night I went to bed with the uncomfortable knowledge that until I had surgery the cancer would continue to grow. I felt desperate to get this thing out of me. I lay awake for hours, tossing and turning, anxious for the morning so I could embark on my new challenge—the challenge of surviving. I knew that every decision I was about to face was serious, with no room for error. I'd thought being a barrister was stressful but nothing could compare to the real stress I was feeling, and the stress that lay ahead.

At the age of thirty-six I was staring down the barrel of my mortality, which can be a lonely and scary experience. You start to question a lot of things. I wondered about my spirituality and began to think more and more about where I'd end up if I didn't make it. It felt like I had caught a bus on my own, the destination bringing only tears. I was frantically trying to disembark at every stop, bargaining the terms of my life. I thought more and more about God and would negotiate regularly. Oh God, I promise I will never eat sugar again, or smoke again, or anything else that can be blamed for putting me in this predicament. What had I done; how had I inadvertently bought this ticket?

I desperately wanted to send my body back to the maker for repairs. I wasn't ready for everything to end in tears. My boys needed me, and I had just bought half a dozen pairs of new shoes in Hong Kong that I wanted to wear.

I spent the next five days trying to find the right surgeon. I was looking for a doctor with a good track record who wasn't knife happy and would not chop me up within an inch of my life. I eventually chose the first surgeon I was referred to. Doctor O'Keck was revered by his colleagues and considered to be the best. One doctor told me that if I was his sister he would only send me to this doctor.

I felt safe with Doctor O'Keck. The other surgeons I went to see were general surgeons whereas he specialised in the operation I needed. One of my concerns was that I'd need a permanent colostomy bag. I knew that I'd require a temporary one; there was no getting around that as the wound would take time to heal. But every other surgeon told me there was a good chance I'd need it permanently. Doctor O'Keck, however, reassured me that I wouldn't. I told him that if he turned out to be wrong, then he needed to make sure the bag was by Prada or Gucci.

We talked at length about the procedure and I told him all my fears—that my body would be scarred for life; that I wouldn't be able to have another baby … But Doctor O'Keck reassured me that the cancer was in its early stages and that I wouldn't need chemotherapy or radiation and he said that I should be able to have another child in the future.

A few days later I was booked for surgery. I knew I would be in hospital for at least two weeks so, to Bettina's bemusement, I had my hair and nails done. I wasn't about to fall apart.

The night before being admitted to hospital was the hardest of all. I was terrified. I had never had surgery and knew this was going to be severe. Friends and family came over to keep me company. Inside, I was verging on hysteria but somehow managed to remain calm and quiet. I didn't want anyone to know how I was feeling. For the first time in my life I took a sedative to sleep.

The following day I arrived at the hospital. As part of the prep for the operation, thick black texta was drawn all over my belly to mark the places for incision. Glancing down, I could see that I was going to be cut from my ribs down to my pelvic bone and across. It looked like I was about to be drawn and quartered. I took some comfort in knowing that a plastic surgeon I'd consulted about the scarring had written to my surgeon to advise him of the best way to stitch up the wound to minimise tissue damage. But I also felt a bit guilty about my vanity. A friend of mine had passed away recently from cancer. During the operation, her surgeon could see that she wasn't going to make it. He stitched her back together rather carelessly, as though there were no need for preservation. He gave her six months to live.

I was afraid the same thing might happen to me. I knew that until the surgeons opened me up, they wouldn't know the severity of the situation. I certainly didn't want to get stitched back together like a sack ready for disposal.

Sitting on the edge of that hospital bed, staring at the texta on my stomach, I was deep in shock. Blank and numb. Was this really happening? I felt like I was in a nightmare. What if I didn't survive? I hadn't said goodbye to my boys. I hadn't said goodbye to anyone. I couldn't have said goodbye; that would have been an admission of defeat and I was determined to survive. I had worked too hard for it to all be over so soon.

The last time I'd faced a serious crisis was at the end of Year Eleven when my mother left. I had dealt with that challenge by being defiant and rebellious. But back then I'd had choices. This crisis offered no choices at all: it was life or death, and it wasn't up to me. The only choices I'd had were surgeons and treatment. I had to figure out a way to cope.

I thought about faith being the opposite of fear. I had to believe that I would survive. I had to have an enormous measure of faith to stay calm. I had to be fearless. Whatever happened, I had to trust that either death or life would be my ultimate healing. I just really, really, really preferred the latter.

I had requested that only my husband be with me when I was admitted to hospital. I didn't want any other family or friends to come as I had to stay focused. I didn't want anyone else to witness me not coping as I knew that I'd have to counsel them through the experience, and I didn't have it in me. I was barely coping myself.

I sat there on my own, waiting for my husband to turn up, distressed and starving as I'd been fasting in preparation for the operation. Finally, my husband arrived two hours later than he had promised to come. I knew he'd been stalling, he was not looking forward to this journey either. I wish he'd told me though, I would have arranged for someone else to be with me rather than sitting on my own.

It seems he wasn't coping very well with his fear. He hated seeing me in this state and couldn't wait to get out of my room. I realised then that men are like mascara: at the first sign of emotion, they run.

The following day I was ready for surgery. As I was wheeled into theatre, my mother, my husband and one of my cousins were there waiting. It was time to say goodbye. Mum looked at me with anguish in her eyes. Her face was purple, as if she'd been holding her breath and was about to pass out. She couldn't talk. Her words were locked behind a lump in her throat. I looked at her; I could see her pain. I knew what she was feeling. I'm a mother, and it was obvious that she wasn't coping. I kissed her on the cheek and could feel her holding her breath. 'Mum, snap out of it,' I said. 'If you believe I'm going to survive you can't fall apart like this.'

Here I was, about to be wheeled into theatre, but counselling her. I knew that if I didn't, she'd lose the strength I needed her to have. She needed to have her act together; I needed to know she would be there for me. If I couldn't fight, she would have to fight on my behalf.

My mother looked at me in shock. She could see my strength and my courage. Quickly composing herself she said, 'Of course you're going to get through this. I love you. I will be waiting here when you get back.'

Seven hours later, I was wheeled into the recovery room. My cousin had supported my mother during the long wait. My husband had smoked a kilo of tobacco and chewed his nails down to a stump. As I was wheeled into the room he was surprised to hear me laugh and talking in my sleep as I seemed to be in a lot of pain. Later he asked me who I was talking to and why I was laughing, but I had no recollection of this, and no idea what he was talking about.

I certainly wasn't laughing because I felt good. I had been cut from one side to the other, forty lymph glands and thirty centimetres of tissue removed. There was an epidural in my back with bags, tubes and wires hanging off me. My mother's face was strained with exhaustion and worry. Her first comment was how beautiful I looked; that with my pink skin, I looked just as I had as a baby. She had seen me wheeled into theatre looking grey and ravaged with disease, but when I returned I no longer had it. In fact, as soon as the cancer was removed, my eyes were clear and my skin glowed. My health had been restored. Of course, I needed to recover from the operation, but the cancer was gone. At the time, I still didn't know whether I would survive; no-one ever does. I had to wait for the pathology results.

I was in hospital for fourteen days and spent the first few days in intensive care recovering from the trauma of surgery and a huge loss of blood. I was in a lot of pain and I could barely move.

Every morning at 7 am a doctor would visit and shove the side of my bed to wake me. I'd seen this doctor six months prior to surgery. He had failed to detect the cancer and I had called to let him know that I wouldn't be coming in for a review appointment because the problem had been detected. I told him that I was having surgery and which hospital I would be in. It wasn't an invitation for him to visit me but perhaps he felt obliged to stay involved in my case. He really was a nuisance. Every morning, he'd scare the life out of me with that bedside shove and ask, 'How is your mood today?'

Well, apart from the fact that you scared the #### out of me, I wanted to say, How would I know? I just woke up—in shock. I was feeling vulnerable and thought he was extremely insensitive, with a terrible bedside manner. I wished he'd stop coming.

One morning, he didn't come in but rang instead, informing me that he had the pathology results. I was anxious to hear the prognosis so eagerly waited for him to speak. I was feeling optimistic as my surgeon had said the operation went well and he'd removed all the cancer. He had also told me that the cancer was in its early stages and hadn't spread. Without consulting my surgeon, this doctor had taken it upon himself to convey the news.

Very quickly, he said, 'It's not good; you have a Dukes' C cancer. It has spread into lymph glands and you only have a thirty-five per cent chance of surviving. You will need chemotherapy and radiation and you may not survive.'

'Hang on … hang on,' I stammered. 'Why are you telling me this over the phone? Can you at least come in and talk to me?'

'No, you're not my patient,' he said, adding that he was 'too busy'.

You mongrel! I thought. You've been here every morning, waking me up, and now you're too busy. He seemed to take delight in being the bearer of bad news. He was an awful man.

I was too upset to think about him. I buzzed for the nurse and told her what had happened. She was appalled at his conduct. Crying, I asked her to give me a sedative because I wasn't coping with the news. Whatever she gave me knocked me out. I remember waking up snoring really loudly, my mouth open because my nose was blocked from crying. That was pretty Gina, I said to myself. Keep it together.

Mum arrived looking exhausted and traumatised. I asked her if she already knew the pathology results. She said that she hadn't heard, but told me she'd just had a car accident in front of the hospital, colliding into the back of a car at about the same time that I'd heard the news.

My surgeon came in soon after. The nurses had called him because they could see my distress and that I needed someone to explain the results to me. Although he refrained from speaking his mind, it was clear that he wasn't at all impressed with the other doctor breaking the news over the phone. I asked him to tell that doctor to never visit me again.

My surgeon reassured me that the prognosis was not as bad as I had been led to believe. He did confirm that I would need chemotherapy and radiation, and that it was worse than he'd initially thought. He hadn't expected that I'd need treatment post surgery, but the cancer had spread into four lymph glands.

I was desperate to see my boys. Myles had been with his grandmother and Christos with his father. I'd arranged to keep them away from the hospital immediately following the operation as I didn't want them to see me in such a state. They had only ever seen me dressed up and on the move. After a few days they were arguing with my mother to take them to the hospital. She had been trying to keep them away but Christos had got angry and demanded that she bring him and Myles in, saying, 'She's my mother and I want to see her.'

I was given warning about their visit so I asked the nurses to remove all the tubes, wires and drainage bags. I made sure I was made up, although my hair was a bit messy. I still had an epidural in my back so I couldn't walk. I put some ice-cream aside for Myles in an attempt to make the visit pleasant. I was so happy to see them. Myles, who had just started Grade One, had painted me a picture at school which the nurses put up on my wall.

When it was time to go, Myles skipped out of the room towards the lift in the foyer. I was relieved that he was leaving happy. But I later learned that as soon as I was out of earshot, he'd stopped in his tracks, turned to his father and burst into tears. He wasn't fooled about the seriousness of the situation.

I hated that my plan to keep him happy hadn't worked; I didn't want him to worry. I didn't want anyone to worry or be upset. But the situation was out of my control; it was very scary for everyone. One minute I'd been living the life I expected would remain the same forever, and the next I was in hospital fighting for my life. I would almost have preferred to have been hit by a bus. If I survived that, at least all I had to do was focus on recovery. But when it comes to cancer, there's no guarantee of recovery.

I didn't want this to be a chapter of my life. I didn't want this to be part of my children's lives. I didn't want scars on my body or to fear death and the treatment ahead. I didn't want any of it. It was bad luck really and I didn't have a choice: I had to cope.

I left hospital two weeks later wearing high heels, makeup and my hair done. I was relieved to be out of there and looking forward to getting home to my own bed and to my boys who were waiting anxiously for my arrival. I was greeted with big hugs and kisses. Chemotherapy was due to start in two weeks and I was pleased to be having a rest in between. I lay on the couch with a pillow and blanket, my boys on either side of me and BooBoo at my feet. My mother told me BooBoo seemed depressed while I was in hospital. We lay there watching movies until my boys fell asleep.

My first day of chemotherapy was very confronting. I hated that I was introducing poison into my body but knew I had no choice. Throughout my treatment, I constantly worked on coping strategies. It felt like my body was falling apart. My mother suggested a few alternate strategies. She knew that if I felt okay, half the battle was won. She suggested, 'Wake up every morning and think beautiful, feel beautiful and look beautiful.' This was a good philosophy. I had always been focused on my appearance and was starting to worry about the drugs' effect on me. I felt very guarded about my looks; I didn't want to appear as bad as I was feeling. I wanted everyone to be encouraged by my presentation. If I looked good then everyone would feel optimistic and no-one would doubt my recovery. I desperately wanted to live and I wanted everyone to believe that I was going to survive.

So I made 'beautiful' my life motto and continued to groom and preen. And when that motto didn't work, I reverted to my alternative motto of: 'Snap out of it.' And when that failed, I relied on my other favourite quote: 'Loretta, get me the big knife.' The line is spoken by Nicholas Cage in *Moonstruck* and it always made me laugh. Of course I had no plans for the big knife. I'd had enough knives from all the surgery, but the scene gave expression to how melodramatic I felt at times.

In the end, fear and I became close friends, giving me the motivation to survive. At first the fear was overwhelming, which wasn't helpful as I worried that I could easily fall apart. I had known anxiety—fear's best friend—after my first son was born. Fear is your instinct telling you that something is not okay. You need to listen to it, but the trick is not to be governed by it as this can be crippling and debilitating. So I challenged the fear. I used it as a motivator to fight. I told the fear to get off me when it became too hard to handle, and to get behind me when it got in my way. I remained in control and dealt with each day as it came rather than looking at the big picture, which seemed too overwhelming to contemplate. My defiance started to kick in, like it had when I was at school. I was determined to overcome this situation. I was determined to survive.

I spent a lot of time reflecting on how such a thing had happened. I wasn't trying to beat myself up, but I never wanted to get cancer again. I had generally been a healthy woman. There was no history of cancer in my family, so it wasn't genetic, as far as I knew. I wondered whether I'd ingested asbestos when I'd pulled the brick cladding off my house when I was nineteen; I was aware that asbestos causes cancer. Had I burned the candle at both ends for too long? Possibly. I had slowed down since having glandular fever, but I had no idea whether that illness was related to the cancer. Perhaps the damage had already been done?

A diagnosis of cancer brings with it considerable responsibility. I felt responsible for everyone around me and felt the need to constantly reassure them that I was okay. I continued to wear high heels and did my hair and makeup every day.

For a long time I avoided telling anyone at work that I had cancer. I had worked so hard to achieve my goal and I wasn't ready for my career to be over. Having been in practice for only three years, I was still a junior.

As soon as I told one person, word spread like fire and before I knew it everyone knew. It's interesting that in the legal profession, an illness can affect your work. People tend to engage lawyers for their aggression and determination, and illness is perceived as a weakness.

I decided to stay away from work until I'd completed all my treatment, which took another six months. By the time I got back to work it was a few weeks before Christmas. I was pleasantly surprised at how compassionate and caring most people were; I hadn't known what to expect. Over the course of my illness and treatment, a few people had displayed a lack of compassion, were judgmental or were at a loss for appropriate things to say. When I went to the drycleaner one day, he pulled back from me as though I had leprosy. Someone once told me that if I got cancer I must have asked for it. Apparently it's worse for lung cancer patients who are often accused of self-inflicting the cancer, even if they've never been a smoker.

On social media recently, a girl posted a picture of herself at her last chemotherapy session. She'd dressed up for the occasion and had her hair and makeup professionally done. Astoundingly, many of the comments accused her of being a fraud because she wasn't wearing a hospital gown and her hair hadn't fallen out. Clearly, such comments came from people who were naive and had never experienced cancer or treatment—which is lucky for them. It's better not to judge if you don't know the facts. The facts would tell you that chemotherapy is administered to day patients, that it doesn't always require a hospital bed and that not all chemotherapy makes your hair fall out as there are different chemicals for different cancers.

When I started treatment I was told that my hair would not fall out. Unfortunately, it did. The doctors explained that this was because I'd been administered an overdose amount of drugs. After that, they reduced the dose. Looking at the upside, I concluded that at least they'd hit me hard, which made the treatment more likely to work.

Some other comments claimed that the girl looked too well to be a cancer patient. Well, not everyone who has chemotherapy is dying. In fact, the purpose of chemotherapy is to avoid death. It is generally administered after surgery to reduce the chances of a recurrence or spread. Sometimes it's administered before surgery to shrink the tumour. Whatever the case, the point is you should walk a mile in someone else's shoes before you make any judgments.

Most of the people I worked with and encountered along the way responded with a lot of empathy, encouragement and support. But the few people who got it wrong taught me a lot.

I learned that the first thing you should not do is tell a cancer patient any horror stories. I don't know what compels people to share what happened to their next-door neighbour who'd died from dehydration while she was undergoing treatment. Do they think that by sharing their experience, they are showing compassion and understanding?

The second thing I learned is that everybody reacts to fear in a different way. Some people fight; some lie down, overwhelmed; while others like me draw deeply on their faith while managing those other two emotions.

Sometimes it's good enough to say, 'I don't know what to say.' The best way to engage with a person who has cancer is to speak to them with compassion. Ask them how they feel, how they are coping, who is supporting them. Ask if they need your help. Enquire if they are okay. Ask them to tell you how they discovered they had cancer. Most people are open to talking about it and if they're not, they will tell you so.

There are various ways you can help and depending on your role in the person's life, there are different ways of handling the situation. If you're the mother, your job is pretty crucial. There aren't many people who don't want the support of their mother during a crisis. Of course, every case is different and every mother-and-child relationship is different. Some mothers can make the situation worse. I was fortunate to have the full support of my mother. Despite not having lived with her since I was a teenager, and a history of some anger and resentment towards her, she was there for me and my boys one hundred per cent. In fact, she sustained us. She cooked for my family every day while still going to work and visiting me in hospital each day. I don't know how she did it. It was inspiring to watch her operate at such a level of stress, yet not skip a beat.

I recall when I came home from hospital Myles asked me what was for dinner. I told him that Nona had cooked and the tray was in the oven. She cooked roast salmon, roast chicken, roast vegetables, cannelloni—all of it on a tray that she'd deliver for heating up. Upon hearing about the tray, Myles burst out: 'Not that tray again! I hate that bloody tray.' I said 'You don't know what's in it.' And he said 'I don't care, I hate that tray.'

Myles loved his grandmother's cooking; his outburst was merely a protest at the situation. Nona's tray was a symbol that his mum wasn't well and still needed help.

Everyone tried to support me as much as they could. Ben visited me regularly in hospital, as did Dad. I remember Dad sitting at the foot of my bed while I struggled to stay awake. I kept apologising to him, I didn't want him to leave. But every time I roused, I would see him sitting there, watching me sleep. He wasn't going anywhere.

Teresa helped out by looking after Myles most of the time. He would stay at her house for weeks on end. She set up a bed in Orson's room so the boys could sleep together. She looked after him and fed him well. By the time he came home he was chubby, and so was she. Evidently, they'd both been comfort eating. Teresa and I laugh about Myles coming home and talking about the delicious food they'd shared together.

Bettina had been with me the night before I went into hospital, then I didn't see her for a while. She delayed coming to the hospital, dreading the idea of seeing me in pain or unwell. She did take me to a few sessions of radiation. I was pretty exhausted by that stage, onto my fifth month of treatment. I had a surgically implanted pick-line in my arm, which administered a dose of chemotherapy every two minutes from a pack that I wore around my waist. The sound of the fluid being released was quiet, but awful. I couldn't wait to get it off. It was attached for six weeks during which I was also having radiation every day so my family took it in turns to drive me to the hospital. Bettina wanted me to get through this and pushed me to be strong.

My husband spent most days with me when I was in hospital, then he'd go to work leaving the day-to-day treatment to my family and friends. I was okay with that; life goes on. I didn't want him to fall apart. The journey was a team effort.

I was in survival mode. I wasn't happy about being a patient and, like some patients, sometimes I was angry. I hated what was happening. Cancer does not inspire happiness. Like a lot of husbands, he felt obliged to make sure I was happy at all times and sometimes became defensive if his efforts to lift my mood failed.

I had a few complications during treatment. Apart from the overdose of chemotherapy which caused my hair to fall out, I also had pulmonary embolus in my lungs and thrombosis caused by the pick-line in my arm. I suppose when your body has endured so many traumas it doesn't always cope. My hair loss was pretty distressing. I had always had a big hairdo, and still do today. But big hair is difficult to achieve with three strands of hair, so I invested in a hairpiece that seemed to work. I was probably about due for a change of style; I'd had the same hair for years.

Despite the complications, I felt constantly reassured that I was going to survive. I had dreamt about my grandmother a couple of weeks before I was diagnosed. She had passed away two years before at the age of ninety-four. It was sad when she passed; she was the matriarch of our family and had been living with my aunty and her seven children with whom she was very close.

In my dream she came to me in the kitchen and tickled my chin like I was a baby. She looked beautiful. She was

I had dreamt about that painting and that letter even before they existed.

Like most Italians, I was brought up with theories that were shrouded in superstition. I was told that if you dream about someone who has passed away and he or she speaks to you, you're going to die. When I told my aunty about that dream, her first question was, Did she speak to you? I don't know how much I believe in superstition, but the dream certainly was a strange coincidence and if it worked in my favour, well, that was good enough for me.

Everything seemed to be looking positive. There were only a few months left of treatment and one more operation. I couldn't wait for it all to end. Thankfully, I hadn't died from dehydration, nor had I fallen victim to any other horror stories. I knew that I had to keep focused on managing one day at a time.

I underwent a second operation about twelve weeks after the first. This time the operation was much quicker, only about two hours. I woke up in recovery feeling much more alert than the previous time. I wasn't writhing in pain and didn't need to be treated for shock with hot blankets.

As I was being wheeled back to my room, falling in and out of sleep, my husband again asked me, 'Why are you giggling? Who are you speaking to?' It was the same conversation I'd had after the first operation. This time I remembered. I was asking God to tell me if I was going to survive. I felt under threat, like I was in a war zone dodging bullets. I needed to know. In my dream, I was standing on a stage talking to hundreds of people, and all of us were laughing. It felt like a vision of my future—that I was going to survive and that at some point in my life I would be on a stage entertaining an audience.

I had many dreams during my surgery and treatment. I guess I was processing a lot of information and obviously felt preoccupied with what was happening to me. I don't usually remember my dreams, nor do I pay much attention to them. But I did end up surviving, and I did end up on a stage, entertaining an audience of hundreds of people.

I completed treatment later that year, deeply relieved that it seemed to have worked. My boys were so happy to have me back. No more 'bloody trays' from Nona and no more hospital for a while. Over the next five years I had regular check-ups, every six months initially, then every year. I constantly worried about a recurrence or a secondary cancer, so I changed my diet and became vigilant about my health. I was told that the next five years would be the hardest given that this was the timeframe in which the cancer could recur or spread.

Five years later I was sitting in a salon getting my nails done when my surgeon called. The previous day I'd had my regular blood test and a procedure to investigate the cancer site for signs of a recurrence. I'd reached the five-year mark and I'd been waiting anxiously all day for his call. I knew that these results would indicate whether I was cured.

'Gina, I've got all your results,' he said.

'Yes?' I replied, holding my breath.

'Good news, they're all clear.'

I was speechless, I started to cry. It was an unexpected reaction. I wasn't aware of how much stress I had been carrying, waiting to hear that five-year result.

The doctor went on to say, 'I suppose this is good news, you've reached the five-year mark so it looks like you're cured and don't have to worry about a recurrence or metastases.'

It was the best news I had ever heard. Cells are rejuvenated in cycles and after five years, if the cancer doesn't recur, it's a good indication that it is well and truly gone. Thank God.

I made a hundred phone calls and sent messages to family and friends to share the good news. That night, my whole family went out for dinner to celebrate, including my boys, my mother, my sisters, my brothers, nieces and nephews.

The next step was reaching the ten-year mark. That would put me in the same category as the rest of the population in terms of cancer risk.

I reached the ten-year mark in 2013 and celebrated that milestone by hosting a 'girls' night in' in support of the Cancer Council of Victoria. It's an annual fundraiser where girlfriends come together and donate the same amount of money they would spend if they'd gone out for the night. The event was filmed and featured in season one of *The Real Housewives of Melbourne* in which I discuss writing this book and this chapter specifically. I wanted to know how many had been touched by cancer and the sorts of thing they would like to read in my book. All the women had been touched by cancer, not just through meeting me but through family and friends. They were interested in reading about my experience so they could understand, firsthand, what happens through such a journey. I'm hoping this chapter has provided some insight.

Since then, I have become an ambassador to the Cancer Council of Victoria, supporting their charity events, spreading awareness and raising funds for cancer research.

A Single Mother's Journey (2005–2015)

T HE YEARS 2003 and most of 2004 were largely taken up with cancer treatment and recovery. In late 2004, my husband and I sold one of our houses to alleviate the financial burden caused by a year off work and exorbitant medical expenses. We had a lot of money left over so we took the boys on a world trip, hoping to shift the focus from the trauma of the previous two years. We travelled to Italy, England, New York and Japan, and it was a wonderful holiday: just what we all needed. On our return, we moved into our new house, which was beautiful with a swimming pool, high ceilings, parquetry floors, marble kitchen and bathrooms, open fireplaces and balconies. Summer was on its way and we were all optimistic.

We had a solid income from renting out the townhouse next door and our previous home so I didn't need to rush back to work; however, I'd never planned to leave my career so I returned to practice in late 2003 and by 2004 I was working most days. It took me a while to get back into the swing of things but I was just so relieved to have put that awful cancer journey behind me. My hair was growing back, albeit slowly, and by the end of 2004 I stopped wearing hairpieces—although my hair was still pretty short and looked a bit damaged. But I didn't care; I was just happy to be alive.

I worked hard as a barrister and enjoyed every minute of it; it was challenging and rewarding. I felt that I had made the right decision about my career: I was exactly where I wanted to be. In general, life was going well. My boys were happy, I was a loving and devoted mother, and my marriage was intact. We went away most weekends to the beach or country, and took road-trips interstate. Life was good.

As part of my recovery, I was having weekly vitamin C infusions which meant being on a drip for about an hour. I was trying to restore my immune system after the hammering it had copped from chemotherapy. I was still worried about a possible recurrence so I was vigilant about my regular blood tests and exploratory day procedures every six months. I started eating organic food and went to bed early.

This was a far cry from the girl who'd worked through the night and had once functioned on three hours' sleep. I had certainly learned a lot about burning out and wasn't going to let that happen again. I found my stop button and used it regularly. After all, I had achieved what I'd needed to, and now it was time to start enjoying the fruits of my labour.

A few months after we moved into the new house I started looking for my next development project. We were financially established and ready to upgrade. I always checked the street where I grew up. It's on the golden mile in Brighton and houses for sale don't come up very often as most people who live there aren't planning to move. Nevertheless, I didn't give up hope of returning there one day.

Eventually I found a house. It was a corner house, not the same corner as the house of my childhood but across the road, which was even better as it was beachside. I remember as a child watching the house being constructed from my bedroom window; the vendors were the same people who'd built it in the seventies. Their children had grown up there but by now all had moved out and the couple was ready to move into something smaller around the corner but still on the beach. The house was for private sale as the vendors didn't want the inconvenience of an auction, preferring the agent to sift through prospective buyers and eliminating a parade of sticky-beaks and nosy neighbours.

I inspected the house one sunny afternoon. I loved it; it was perfect. I was looking to buy with the intention to pull it down and rebuild. I called my architect and we quickly worked out that we could fit two houses on the block. This formula had worked so far and I was going to stick to it.

We bought the house. I had enough money in the bank to put down a substantial deposit, and settlement was arranged for thirty days. We had enough equity in our other homes to secure a loan to develop the property. I couldn't believe that I was finally returning to my old street; I had dreamt of this for years. I was excited about building my dream home as well as having a lucrative investment property next door.

By late 2004, I felt that my life was back on track. However, despite surviving cancer, travelling the world, moving house and buying my dream home, my husband and I were still arguing. During cancer treatment I took on the role of counselling everyone around me; but this was difficult to sustain with my husband as we were together constantly. He witnessed my lows and my extra lows. I had to stay focused on getting through every day and meeting every challenge. He didn't cope very well. He withdrew and became distant. I think he feared losing me and didn't know how to handle this. His reaction upset me and we argued a lot during this time.

Despite my return to health, our relationship didn't really recover; evidently, the damage had been done and our marriage came to an end. After fifteen years together, one day he said to me that he 'didn't want to be responsible for whether I lived or died'. I was deeply shocked at his words. Apart from the fact that he wasn't, in fact, responsible for my life, he seemed to neglect that a husband is supposed to care. The stress of our relationship was compounding the stress of my cancer treatment, thereby affecting my recovery, so I told him he didn't have to stay and that he could go, which he did.

We separated in mid-2005. We tried to reconcile several months later, but it just didn't work. I had re-acquainted with a guy I'd known for many years and my husband insisted there was something more between us. Although there was no romantic element to this friendship, I severed the friendship in the hope of preserving my family life. I tried really hard to work things out with my husband, even calling my father to come and talk to him, but nothing worked. He was blinded by jealousy and convinced that the marriage was over. My father wasn't impressed and simply said, 'What a-you gonna do? Let him a-go.' So I let him go.

I was on my own again with my boys. I couldn't believe that after investing so much in a fifteen-year relationship, it had failed. I was thirty-eight and had been with my husband since I was twenty-five. I was shocked that he hadn't fought for the marriage and that he left after he'd seen me struggle through cancer treatment, and he knew that I still wasn't well. I was deeply disappointed that he didn't have the courage to stay. I didn't know whether I'd get through the next five years, and neither did he.

I worried about my boys and how they would cope with the break-up and not having their father around. Christos had been eighteen months old when we started living together, so the two of them were very close. I felt that my boys had been through enough trauma and I really wished it hadn't come to this; but I also knew that I could look after them, even though my health was compromised. And I did.

In 2006, a year after separation, the boys and I moved into the house on the beach. It wasn't my dream home yet but the location was perfect. I still intended to develop the site—the architectural designs were ready and I had been granted the building permits—but I had to put the plans on hold now that I was on my own as my husband had stopped contributing to the household and his children after we separated, he was unemployed so there was nothing to chase.

The house was unrenovated but comfortable. The previous owners were Italian, so the house had a very Italian feel which the boys liked. It had heated floors and three bedrooms upstairs. The carpet was a bit threadbare and the bathrooms needed renovating, but we settled in very happily. In fact, my boys have said that it was their favourite house.

I set up a shared study and games room for them upstairs, which offered views of the bay through a floor-to-ceiling window. Myles was in Grade Five and Christos in Year Ten.

As part of my marriage settlement I organised the sale of our other properties except this one; I loved the location and still planned to develop the site. But then I realised that even if the redevelopment happened years later, my husband could still come back and claim some of the equity. This was very frustrating since I was the one servicing the loan, and I was raising the boys without any contribution from him. To my great disappointment, I felt that I had no choice but to sell. Despite it being the house I'd spent years searching for, I needed to sever ties with my husband and get on with my life. In 2007, I found a developer who was keen to buy the property with the plans and permits; he could start the project immediately.

In mid-2007, I bought another house and we moved in on my forty-first birthday. This house was on the beach about three-hundred metres away from the old green weatherboard home where I'd lived with my sisters during my final years at school. I could still picture Honey running up and down the street. In some ways, I felt like my mother: living in the same street, a single mother with four children—although two of mine were canine, our dogs Pepsi and BooBoo.

Our new home was beautiful: it had practically just been built, comprising three storeys with bay views. It had a similar feel to the houses I had built in the past so it felt like home and we loved living there. Although we'd moved house a lot, my boys didn't really care where we lived as they said, 'Mum will always make it comfortable.' My bedroom was upstairs, as was the living room which overlooked the beach. The downstairs area was the boys' domain with their bedroom and ensuite on that level; they loved the freedom and independence this set-up gave them.

I continued to host parties and would cook for days, celebrating with family and friends. My boys and I had a tremendous relationship and I loved being their mother; they were, and still are, beautiful boys.

We lived in that house for a few years. I continued to work full-time at the bar and was doing well. I loved living in the area where I grew up, and every night after dinner I'd go for a walk along the beach. I didn't miss being married. In fact, life felt very peaceful without a partner who tended to frustrate me. I was financially independent and my boys were happy.

I started dating the guy my husband had suspected me of seeing. Although we'd known each other for many years, I never imagined I'd ever go out with him as I considered him as a friend only. He'd been married for twenty years and had three children to that marriage.

I hadn't seen him for years and by chance I ran into him the day I separated from my husband. I had left the house briefly to get a coffee and there he was in the cafe. I told him my news, but I didn't explain the circumstances of my separation. Following that chance encounter, we remained friends.

The following year my friend's marriage ended and he moved out of his family home. We started spending more time together. We were both single and over time we became romantically involved. We are still together today. Our relationship was founded on a long-term friendship and we have managed to stay together through thick and thin. Our friendship instilled an appreciation of who we are as individuals, and we developed a mutual respect for each other. We are both parents, we both work hard, we have the same energy, the same values and we love each other. I have often said that I operate at my best when I'm in love so I was confident that the years to come would be good.

I retained some sadness that my marriage hadn't lasted and that my husband wasn't with me to celebrate my full recovery from cancer. It wasn't so much that I wanted him there—he was annoying me by this stage—but it was more a general disappointment that my marriage hadn't weathered the storm despite my belief that the relationship would last forever. After that final separation, there was never any chance at reconciling. I find that most ex-partners never fail to remind you of why you're no longer together, and if you allow it they will confirm this daily. Moreover, I had moved on and was in a new relationship.

As well as shouldering the financial responsibility of ensuring that my children were housed, clothed and fed, it was my job to teach them about life. I didn't want them to be affected by the trauma of cancer or the disruption of separation. Of course, the fact that these things had happened was unavoidable, but I tried to find the meaning. I told my boys that their father's leaving was not about them; that he loved them, and despite not being a great husband, he was still a wonderful father. I also taught them to be resilient and level-headed, to always think before speaking, and that in life you have to keep moving; you can't sit still and contemplate forever.

I didn't want my boys to grow up superstitious or to be afraid. I wanted them to be fearless. In fact, I've never known them to be afraid or hesitant. They've always slept with their door closed and the lights off, comfortable to go to the bathroom in the middle of the night by themselves, unlike me as a child.

The only time I taught them that fear was good was in regards to drugs. I wasn't sure how to address the issue of drugs with them. I was well aware that recreational drug use was out there and pretty common amongst school kids. So when each of my sons was around twelve years of age, I took them aside and asked them what they knew about drugs. At this age, I knew they were still innocent enough to have the conversation without the topic inspiring rebellious behaviour. Each of them told me that they hadn't encountered drugs as none of their friends were using them. I then asked if they knew why people took drugs. They didn't know so I explained that different drugs create different feelings— some make you happy, some make you relaxed and others make you think you are hallucinating. Curious, they asked me why people would want to feel like that. So I explained that some people want to escape their reality, and some just take drugs for fun.

I went on to say that it doesn't matter why people take drugs, or what they take. There is one thing all drugs have in common: all drugs give you a feeling of euphoria, which is, in fact, the onset of death. Each of them gave me the same bewildered look, even though these conversations were years apart. I explained, 'Euphoria is the onset of death because if you have enough of the drug you will die, and this is the start of the dying process.' They were horrified.

That story—along with the pressure of knowing that if anything happened to them my life would be over—created the perfect combination of control through fear and guilt.

My boys were always amused when I tried the Italian mother's way of control—guilt and fear.

But I wasn't melodramatic very often. Instead, I tried to instil wisdom and knowledge. I remember saying to Myles when he was in Grade Six that he should always trust his instinct. When he told me that he didn't know what instinct was, I explained that instinct is the feeling you get to either do, or not do, something. Like when to cross the road or when to trust someone. He was about to leave for school camp that day and was reluctant to participate in one of the activities. I told him to decide once he got there, and if he didn't feel right about doing it, he should tell his teacher. Most people will not challenge your instinct because it's usually a measure of your capacity. Not everyone has the same skills or ability, and if you sense you're going to get hurt, you're probably right.

My theory on parenting has always been to build self-esteem and confidence in my sons. I've encouraged them to feel intelligent and capable and always gave them some responsibility in making decisions while still guiding them through. Adolescence is a difficult time. I dealt with mine by rebelling against my circumstances and aiming for success. But not all teenagers are like this. Most are angry and defiant and push their parents away. After a childhood of constantly being told what to do, they reach a stage when they want to make their own decisions and not follow their parents' orders. Unfortunately, with independence comes a lot of responsibility with limited insight or foresight. Despite feeling like adults, they haven't experienced enough to know how to make the right choices all the time, and are often put in situations where they have to think on their feet.

I talked to my boys at length about how they were feeling at different stages of their childhood and adolescence. I let them know that frustration is a normal emotion and that they should never lose their sense of humour or their self-respect. I reminded them every day that they were loved and gave them plenty of space. I never entered their room without knocking and I never gave them orders. I always asked for their viewpoint and involved them in decision-making.

I've wanted to raise boys into men who can close their eyes at night and have a sense of peace and optimism; who feel loved and believe in themselves; who are responsible for themselves and, to some degree, feel responsible for the people around them. I didn't know how long I would be around and whether they would have to cope without me so I worked hard to make sure that whatever happened, they'd be capable and resilient, and never feel despair or without hope.

In early 2012, I had the unfortunate experience of witnessing a young man try to take his life by jumping off a bridge. It was about one o'clock in the morning and I had just picked up Myles and a friend from a party. I noticed a man was standing on the railing preparing to jump. Cars continued to drive by, and no-one stopped.

I veered across four lanes of traffic, slammed the car into park and ran over to him while dialling 000. 'Hey, hey, you're going to hurt yourself!' I yelled.

He looked at me with terror in his eyes and said, 'I'm going to jump.'

I looked down to see where he would land. 'You're not going to like that,' I remarked. It was a thirty-metre drop onto the road below and there were cars travelling directly beneath us. I had a vision of him landing on a car as it drove innocently by, and that he might take the passengers with him.

I put my hand up, gesturing for him to take it, then rubbed the back of his arm and tugged on the sleeve of his t-shirt saying, 'Come and talk to me.' It was a tricky situation as I didn't want him to accidentally fall or do anything impulsive. I knew that I was taking a risk as he could be very unstable and if he was willing to kill himself, he mightn't care what happened to me. But despite my fear and racing pulse, I persevered. He stepped down and looked at me.

'Where have you been tonight?' I asked him.

He told me he'd been out with friends.

'Where are they now?' I asked, thinking it strange that his friends had left him in such a fragile state. I asked whether he'd been drinking or taking drugs. He said he'd had a few drinks with his friends. I was trying to gauge who I was dealing with. I noticed that he had an accent and enquired where he was from. When he told me he was from Ireland, I asked what he was doing in Australia.

'I'm working as a chippy,' he said.

'A chippy?' I said, mimicking his accent, 'What's a chippy?'

He smiled, and I thought: got you! That's all I needed— to see a smile. I asked where his mum was and he answered that she was back in Ireland. He told me he had brothers and sisters back home.

I said to him, 'You know people do love you.'

He looked at me with a perplexed expression.

'I love you,' I said, 'and I don't even know who you are. Look at your beautiful body that your mother nurtured. I'm a mother and I know what that means.'

As I said that, Myles got out of the car with his friend. I looked over and pointed, 'That's my son over there, I said. 'I've always told him that if anything ever happened to him my life would be over, no pressure.'

The young man smiled again. I thought, Thank God, I might be getting through to him. He told me that he was twenty-eight years old and that his head hadn't been right. I reassured him that every day is different and that we've all felt like our head wasn't right at some stage. I told him that at twenty-eight, he was a baby; that he hadn't lived his life. 'You haven't even met the people who mean something to you, you haven't met the people you are going to love and who will love you in return,' I said.

He was coming around. His body language was more relaxed and some colour was returning to his face. The eye contact between us was pretty intense.

Suddenly the police arrived, sirens blaring. He looked shocked. Aware of how fragile he was, I told him that I had called the police just before I got to him. 'Please don't worry,' I reassured him, 'I promise you're not in trouble. I just wanted to make sure you were alright. They just want to make sure you're alright. Trust me,' I said, 'I'm a lawyer.' Oh my God, I'd been doing so well; where did that cheeseball comment come from? Fortunately, he understood my intentions, and was amused rather than put off.

The police spoke to the young man and led him to their van. I told him he should go with them, knowing they would get him to a hospital. He hugged me and gave me a kiss on the cheek. I hugged him back and reassured him that he shouldn't ever beat himself up for feeling like he had, and that he should take comfort in knowing that every day brings a fresh start.

I never saw or heard of him again. I hoped he was okay and said prayers for him. Contemplating how close his mother had come to losing her son gave me chills. Love can sometimes conquer all.

When I arrived home that night with Myles and his friend, I was still shaky and chilled to the bone. Christos was at home, watching TV on the couch.

'Christos!' Myles said, 'Mum just saved some guy from jumping off a bridge, she saved his life!'

'Oh, okay,' he said, and went back to watching TV. Myles laughed at him.

'Doesn't he believe you?' I asked Myles.

'Yes, he believes me, but we are used to you helping people so he's not surprised.'

I pondered his comment and realised that over the years my boys have seen me talk to people in the street, give them money, food and help in any way I could. I hadn't realised they'd been watching, but I hope my actions will leave an enduring impression and that they emulate me when they are adults.

Later that year my partner moved to the USA to follow opportunities in property development. It was a difficult situation. I didn't want him to go but in life you've got to respect people's decisions and sometimes you just have to let them go. I wasn't sure what this meant for our future. I knew I couldn't and wouldn't leave my boys to go and live with him. We had never lived together as I preferred my set-up with my boys, and didn't want our relationship to interfere with our household dynamic. So we embarked on a long-distance relationship. We spoke every day, I travelled to the USA every few months and he came home fairly often. We were only ever apart for a month or two, but still, it was difficult and unsettling. I didn't know where the relationship was heading and I wasn't sure whether I could sustain the distance and loneliness that came with his absence. But at the same time, I wasn't ready to move on so decided not to worry about being on my own.

It was the first time I had ever been alone and it took me a while to adjust. But I did. I threw myself into work and focused on taking care of my boys. They were growing up so fast and I knew I had only a few more years before they started living independent lives. I spent more time with my family and made a lot of new friends. I didn't know whether I would eventually move on or whether my partner would meet someone else in the States. I hoped that it wasn't over.

As it turned out, it wasn't. He came back to Australia at the end of 2014. We are now living together and hope to stay together forever. I'm glad that I was patient and that we remained in touch—although it would have been difficult to relinquish our contact, as each day I had so much to tell him and we would talk for hours.

In some ways, our relationship evolved to a new level through this daily communication. We had become very close over the years, confiding everything in each other. He is also Italian, so we get it when each of us succumbs to melodrama. He has a big heart that's full of compassion, and he is strong and quick-witted. We share a work ethic as he was also raised by an Italian father who worked very hard. He is a man of courage and is fearless like me. Most of all, he lets me be me. He gives me room to be a woman and never challenges my role as a mother or as someone who needs two hours to get ready in the morning. They say that if a man treats you like a princess, he's been raised by a queen. I think his mother got it right. Interestingly, I had never dated an Italian man, always assuming they'd be difficult. My partner proved me wrong.

I have been a single parent now for ten years. It's been an amazing journey and through it I have experienced a range of emotions—anger, frustration and gratitude. My boys have also learned a lot. They have watched me endure cancer and survive. Their early awareness of mortality has granted them a perspective on life that many young people (fortunately) don't have. I waited for the rebellious teenage years to strike, but the defiance never came. My sons have never argued with me, competed with each other, spoken a nasty word or hassled me for anything. This is either due to my parenting, or perhaps the experience of seeing me endure surgery and treatment knocked out their impulse to rebel. They seem to really trust me, and trust every decision I make—which is always in consultation with them. I don't think I have let them down so far, and I hope I never do.

I always assumed I'd live out my days practising law and never considered shifting focus. But life is full of surprises, as I had learnt, and there were more to come.

CHAPTER EIGHT

A Real Housewife of Melbourne (2012–2015)

I N DECEMBER 2012, I stepped out of court to take a call from Teresa. It was unusual for her to call me during the day so I assumed it must be important. Dad was in a nursing home—he'd had a stroke at seventy-five and now suffered vascular dementia—so we always answered each other's calls immediately.

The call wasn't about Dad; it came from left of field. Teresa told me that two casting agents had come into her shop asking about me. They were casting for a reality TV show and apparently my name had come up several times from various people as a potential candidate. They didn't know how to contact me but were aware that Teresa and I were sisters. Teresa wanted to know if it was okay to pass on my number. She had told them she thought I'd be fantastic in a reality TV role, that I had been through a lot and that I was the sort of girl who looked the part and would make people laugh and cry, sometimes in the same minute. She showed them a photo of me wearing a hot-pink dress with big earrings that had been taken a few weeks before at Orson's birthday party. They said they were definitely interested.

I went home wondering what it was all about. I knew they had mentioned something about housewives, and I was aware of a franchise housewives show on pay TV that I had never watched because the women tended to argue a lot.

The following afternoon I received a call from one of the agents, inviting me to meet them for a coffee. I agreed to meet her and her colleague at the cafe around the corner. I arrived dressed for a twenty-first birthday party I was attending that night. Wearing a pale-blue jewelled dress with a gold keyhole chain neckline and high heels, I certainly did not look like a typical barrister; there was nothing corporate about me.

Smiling at me in greeting, the women told me they were casting for 'The Real Housewives of Australia' and had been searching for cast members for nearly a year, interviewing countless women. They hadn't yet decided where the show would be based, whether it would be in Melbourne, Sydney,

Perth or the Gold Coast. The location would be determined by where the talent was found as the show would only work if they managed to assemble a strong cast.

'Isn't that the show where the women argue a lot and pull each other's hair?' I asked, adding, 'If you want bitchy cat fights you won't get that from me.'

They laughed and explained that they were looking for women who were inspiring. The format of the show, which was unscripted, was to bring six women together and film the interpersonal dynamics and the evolution of their relationships. They certainly weren't looking to cast the type of women who would pull hair out.

At best, I was curious and flattered that they were interested to meet me. They asked if they could film me to assess how I appeared and sounded on screen. They would ask me a number of simple questions, reassuring me that there would be no tricks or traps. Apparently, some people have a great presence off-camera but on-camera they seem to disappear, while others who look quite plain and reserved can blossom on screen. I'm guessing they didn't put me in the quiet, reserved category. Anyone who wears as much eyeliner as I do is definitely not reserved.

The following week the two women came to my home. I was wearing a turquoise dress with twisted shoulder straps, high heels and turquoise gold jewellery with matching blue eyeliner. I'd had a spray-tan and bleached my teeth—just the usual panel-beating, nothing out of the ordinary.

They set up a chair next to the back window in my living room to get as much natural light as possible and started rolling their hand-held camera which wasn't much bigger than an iPhone. I answered the questions, feeling a bit nervous, unsure whether my looks or my responses were more important. I suppose it was all of the above; no pressure.

One of the questions was, 'What is your life's motto?'

'Snap out of it,' I answered. Dad had taught it to me and if only they knew how many times I'd used it.

Another question was, 'If you saw your best friend's boyfriend with another woman, would you tell her?'

I replied, 'Well, seeing him with another woman doesn't mean anything, but if he had his tongue down her throat, then I might need to tell her.'

The women laughed at many of my answers and looked pleased with how I was presenting. I still wasn't particularly interested in what they were casting for, but I was curious enough to go along with it and see where it ended up. The women explained they were compiling a set of screen tests to present to the network. I hadn't thought that far ahead; I certainly hadn't considered that I'd be part of the initial pitch.

As the women left, they told me that I'd done well and that they would get back to me in a few days. They asked whether I'd be interested in attending a lunch with other potential cast members which would be filmed as part of their pilot. They were keen to see how all the women interacted. I agreed to go along.

Christmas came and went. It was a difficult and lonely Christmas that year as it was the first I'd spent without my partner, who was in the USA. Mum hosted it, and as usual she catered for two hundred people even though there were only twenty guests. In the car on the way to Mum's, Myles and I sang songs and discussed the year ahead. 'I wonder where we will be this time next year?' He was starting Year Eleven and I was contemplating life without my partner.

'I think it's going to be a good year, Mum,' he said.

'I think so too,' I agreed, concealing my stress. I had resigned myself to being on my own for a while and it was a big adjustment.

A few weeks after Christmas, I went to Las Vegas to spend some time with my partner. It was a brief but wonderful holiday; I was so happy to see him. Soon after my return, I was scheduled to attend the lunch with the casting agents and the other potential cast members; I had no idea who else would be there or what to expect.

I arrived to find a whole production crew waiting in the wings—cameras, lighting and sound guys. I knew Andrea Moss and two others out of the twelve women, but I had heard of most of them. There were sandwiches, chocolates and champagne. One of the girls quickly started eating the sandwiches before the cameras started rolling. She was a bit chubby and clearly starving, cramming egg sandwiches in her mouth with two hands. Dear Lord, I thought, what are you doing?

The cameras started to roll. We were asked to take a piece of paper out of a bowl, read the question written on it and then each of us had to respond. Most of the girls expressed an opinion on most topics, which was good as it took the pressure off me. Similar casting lunches were held in different states around Australia.

I went home after the lunch and didn't give it too much further thought. I wasn't expecting anything more to come of it. A few weeks later, however, the casting agents rang me again. They wanted to introduce me to one of the other girls they'd been talking to—Lydia Schiavello, whom I'd met about eight years before but with whom I'd lost contact. Lydia and I struck up a new friendship and spoke frequently during the casting process.

I went overseas again in March 2013 and stayed with my partner who'd set up an apartment in Atlanta. While there, I received a phone call from the casting agent. The broadcaster who'd commissioned the show had settled on their cast and had agreed to film it in Melbourne; it was going to be called The Real Housewives of Melbourne. They had selected six women and I was one of them.

I was quite surprised to have been chosen; I'd never thought of myself on television. I was aware that I had quite a unique style and look, and that I could be entertaining, but felt nervous at the prospect of a large audience. So I was in two minds about whether to accept. Was I really interested in having cameras at my place, invading my space?

I forwarded the agreement they'd sent me to my lawyer and when I came back to Australia I entered further negotiations. I hadn't considered how much time it would take to produce the show and the extent of its impact on my legal career. I would have to take time off and I was concerned about how the show might affect my credibility. I knew the opportunity could be life-changing, but I didn't know whether it would be in a good or a bad way. Would I become famous? With fame comes a lot of responsibility, and I could lose my privacy. People would recognise me and I worried how the exposure would affect my boys.

By early July, I had to make some firm decisions. I was formally offered the role and given the contact to sign. Still, I was undecided. I had to be comfortable with the terms of the contract and I wanted the producers to reveal all the cast members. I was aware that Lydia, Andrea and Janet had been selected—Janet I'd known for over twenty years—but the other two women were a mystery. The producers wanted it to be a surprise, but I felt it was important to know. After all, I had to work with these women and was concerned whether they were people with whom I wanted to be associated.

I wasn't entirely happy with the terms offered and, being the lawyer I am, I continued to negotiate. Ultimately, all the women would be bound by the same contract so I knew that every term I negotiated would benefit the whole team. Three of the cast members and I had the same lawyer. I started consulting our lawyer to settle the terms. I sat with her for a total of nineteen hours over a two-week period until we got it right. Even then, I remained unsure about whether I'd sign up.

The deadline came. It was time to sign. I went to bed the night before, still in two minds about what to do. I asked my boys for their opinion. In their usual way, they told me they trusted me to make the right decision. But this didn't really help because I wasn't sure what the right decision was. I had an appointment with my solicitor at ten o'clock the following morning so I tossed and turned all night. I recalled my dream when I came out of surgery in which I was laughing and entertaining an audience. Was it a premonition? I certainly hadn't chased that vision; in fact, until now I had forgotten about it. But it seems it was chasing me.

I pondered whether I was taking it all a bit too seriously and started to play it down. Perhaps the show would only be on pay TV and hardly anyone would watch it, I thought. But I had to consider its impact on my career. I had put considerable effort and many years of hard work into achieving my goal; I didn't want to ever risk ruining it. I had mentioned the prospect of the show to several colleagues. One agreed that probably no-one would watch it, another thought it would be fun, while another had watched the shows in the USA and was really excited, encouraging me to sign up. I had worked with this particular colleague for over ten years and she'd seen me in court on many occasions. She thought I was intelligent and quick-witted enough to be entertaining, telling me, 'Just do it, you'll kill it.'

But what was I going to kill? That was the question. I felt quite burdened by the decision: to sign or walk away. It was all being handed to me but I wasn't sure whether I wanted it. I worried that if the show failed, or if I failed on the show, it would affect my practice and I didn't have a fall-back position, unlike many of the women, who had their husbands as a safety net. For me, however, there was no room for error. I couldn't put my boys at risk. I had a busy practice, we had a good life together and were comfortable. Did I really need to complicate things?

I spoke to my partner at length about my dilemma. He encouraged me to do whatever I wanted to do. I explained my concerns, which he understood, and he acknowledged that it wasn't an easy decision. He pointed out that the show could offer me further opportunities—although for what, I wondered? I supposed it might be a platform to launch into other things; but then, it could also be a platform for disaster. My reputation was based on credibility and intelligence; would I ruin my profile? I hadn't chased fame or celebrity status, ever.

The other significant issue was that signing the contract would tie me to the filming schedule for weeks to come, preventing me from visiting my partner overseas. I was barely coping with our month on, month off routine and I knew that fourteen or fifteen weeks of filming would require him to come home to see me. I wasn't sure whether he could do that. Instead of thinking 'absence makes the heart grow fonder', I was thinking 'out of sight, out of mind' and that the time apart would give him more of an opportunity to move on.

I spoke at length to my mother and my sisters. Bettina said I should just 'go for it' and Teresa thought I should do it because I was entertaining and hilarious; she'd been hearing my jokes and one-liners since childhood.

On the morning I was due to sign, I was still unsure. Having work-shopped it with everyone, it was now up to me to make the final decision. I rang Teresa on the way to the meeting. She could hear the tension in my voice and suggested that the whole thing was causing too much stress and perhaps I should just withdraw. I felt relieved that someone had given me an out and would understand if I walked out of the meeting empty-handed.

I entered the office. The contract was sitting on the table with nothing around it aside from a pen. My solicitor left the room to give me time to think. I rang the producers and asked for the names of the other two cast members, which they'd promised to reveal upon signing of the contract. They told me the girls' names; they were right: I hadn't heard of them. I quickly did a Google search and thought they looked nice enough. One was a psychic and the other was married to the sandwich king of Melbourne. I thought I could cope with that. My excuses were diminishing.

I rang my partner in the USA; it was late in the evening and he was having dinner with friends. Once again, I explained my dilemma and that I was concerned the obligations of the contract would make it impossible for me to visit him for weeks.

'What have you got to lose?' he said.

'A lot.'

'Just go for it,' he encouraged. It was the first time he'd given me a definitive answer as previously he'd just listened to my concerns.

'You know I will always look after you,' he said, 'and in the worst-case scenario, if you botch things up, you can come and live with me in the States.'

That's true, I thought, I have an out. And even if I don't live in the US full-time because of my boys, I could travel back and forth to be with him.

Pen in hand, it was time to decide. I thought again about my dream, and that until now I had always been fearless. So, with my innate spirit of adventure, my faith and my fearless attitude, I signed.

A few weeks later we started filming. My first day was at my house; my boys and I were filmed while I prepared a plate of food. I told them I'd been to the gym. They laughed because they know that I have never been to a gym, and were amused to hear me explain that I have muscly arms from back-combing my hair. We filmed a few more scenes that day which would be used as back-story to introduce me to the audience. It was fun, but exhausting. I was a novice and so were the boys. Early that morning, a girl had arrived to take care of hair and makeup, although I declined the offer to do my makeup. In retrospect, I probably should have let her; I might have looked a little less like I had fallen into a vat of Crayola, to quote a friend, with whom I laughed when the show went to air.

Once the crew had left, I lay on the couch exhausted; I think I fell asleep. Myles looked at me and said, 'What happened to you?' We laughed together. I had been so attentive all day and now I had collapsed within five seconds of the crew leaving. I hoped I'd get used to this quickly; I really didn't want to make a habit of falling asleep sitting up.

A few days later we filmed in chambers. I was robed and wigged. I hadn't filmed with the girls yet which was good in a way as it gave me an opportunity to find my feet. All I needed to do was be myself and let the world see me as I am.

My first filming with the girls was the first time the viewers saw us all together. As I've mentioned, the show is not scripted so I really did meet Jackie and Chyka, the other two cast members, on that night. A week later, the girls caught up for a publicity shoot. Within twenty-four hours the cast was announced to the world and the images were all over the papers and social media. There was an instant buzz of excitement out there. I received calls and messages from people I hadn't seen for years: girls I went to school with, neighbours of distant relatives that I had never met, people I couldn't remember.

I wondered how judges and magistrates were receiving the news; I hoped they'd be open-minded. I had been appearing in their courts for fourteen years and they knew me well. Later I heard that the publicity photo for the show was proudly on the wall in their tea-room. I certainly wasn't the first barrister to branch out into the field of entertainment; in fact, many could be described as frustrated actors. We always have an audience and try to be entertaining—at least to the point of keeping everyone awake during a trial.

We filmed for sixteen weeks from July 2013, and by December we had season one. It was an absolute rollercoaster ride and I was so relieved when it was over. I had worn eighty-five different outfits in sixteen weeks, which was an achievement in itself. My hair hurt from all the blow-waves and my feet needed a rest. As well as filming for hours most days, I was still going to court. I hadn't really discussed the show with my colleagues, but they seemed excited to watch it when it went on air.

Once filming ended, I tried to get back to my normal life. I knew there would be a lot of publicity, interviews and photo shoots leading up to the premier. We didn't know the date it would screen so I went into the new year excited and anxious about the direction my life would take.

I was back in court early in the new year, knowing that it was only a matter of time before the promotional billboards went up all over Melbourne. I was aware that the producers had increased their publicity budget—possibly to accommodate my hair on the billboards, I thought. But then I found out that they weren't just using billboards; the show was being promoted on digital billboards, bus stops, buses, coffee cups and magazines. I was everywhere. Messages from friends and family crammed my phone, alerting me to the location of the various billboards and sending me photos of buses with my image plastered on the side. On one occasion, I walked out of court to see my face on a bus parked right outside. I stopped in my tracks and started walking backwards. I turned and fled back into the court, telling my colleagues that I had just scared myself. Here we go, I thought, you can run but you can't hide.

Throughout the month of February the cast travelled around Australia promoting the show. The itinerary was hectic: more outfits and more blow-waves. Most nights I only had a few hours' sleep, followed by long days of radio, magazine and newspaper interviews plus photo shoots. The media was excited and wanted to know everything, but they had to wait for the show to start. I arrived home a few days before the show went to air.

The show premiered on 23 February 2014. My partner flew back from the USA to be with me. All the housewives had seen the first few episodes in a private screening, but I hadn't watched it with anyone else. Countless people invited me to watch the show with them as it went to air. I really wanted to watch it with my boys who wanted to watch it with their friends. But I also really wanted to watch it with my sisters, my mum, my girlfriends and my cousins; this was a new chapter in my life that I wanted to share with the people I'd grown up with. I especially wanted to watch it with my partner, but I knew he didn't want to watch it at Mum's house. The only solution was to hire a venue so we could all watch it together. I wanted to keep it intimate, but when I counted all my family and friends and the boys' friends it amounted to about eighty guests. This felt like too many people but I couldn't get around it; in fact, even more people wanted to come. Despite my efforts, the guest-list grew to over three-hundred-and-fifty guests—and that was after I told guests that the numbers were limited and it was a closed invitation. I would have had a thousand people there if I wasn't vigilant about the numbers.

The guests arrived in droves, all dressed up for the occasion. It was an exciting night. As well as friends, colleagues and family, a few magistrates and judges came. I put together a reel of all the super-8 movies my father had made when I was growing up. Many of my relatives hadn't seen those movies since the 1970s and they loved watching the old footage.

The only person missing was my dad, which I was sad about. He wasn't well enough to attend and he would have been confused by all the goings-on. His memory had deteriorated over the past few years and he was becoming increasingly vague about who we all were. Dementia is a cruel disease. He often mistook Teresa for his own sister, and when I showed him an autograph card with my photo on it, he said, 'That looks like you.' I tried to explain it was me and that I was on television. He became even more confused, not wanting to keep the photo because he felt he had enough photos in his room.

Before the show, I thanked everyone for coming and briefly described what I had been up to in the preceding months. I ended my speech with 'Team Gina!' and gave each person a showbag containing a Team Gina t-shirt (pure cotton, of course) with gold writing, coffee cups with my photo, and other goodies one of my girlfriends had pulled together.

The show began and each time I came on screen the audience cheered and yelled, 'Team Gina!' The newspapers reported the story of the night, headlining the article 'Team Gina' and describing the support I'd received. One of my girlfriends who couldn't attend happened to be working across the road; she told me she could hear the cheering; it sounded like a football match, she said.

Having so much support meant an enormous amount to me. I hadn't had much support from the girls on the show and I had come away feeling stressed about how the world would receive me. I was worried about the editing of the show and that things might be taken out of context. For example, I'm heard to use the word 'moron' but then later I'm heard saying, 'I don't even use that word, moron,' I was explaining the word was peculiar to the girls and it seemed I was denying the use of the word when clearly I had said it.

Every week I watched anxiously as the show went to air. Apparently, the audience kept growing as they waited for the next episode to unfold. I'm told the show became the water-cooler topic of conversation around the nation. I couldn't go anywhere without people discussing the last episode and how they felt about it. I was surprised that the show was so popular; I had thought Australians would be reluctant to embrace a show that was based on an American franchise as we tend to dislike mimicry. But the producers had put together a spectacular program that didn't mimic anything. It was organic and stood out on its own.

I won't bore you with the details of the show's content as most of you have probably watched it; and if you haven't, you might watch it after you've read this book. Suffice to say, the process took a long time and the producers clearly got it right. It was the highest-rating show in the network's history outside of sport, and the audience continued to grow from week to week. Viewers were compelled by the relationships and the dynamics between the six housewives. We were all opinionated women with privileged lifestyles, from different walks of life with different values, different intellectual standards and different worth. But at the end of the day, we were all accustomed to being the boss and it was a case of too many chiefs and not enough Indians. Most of the women were used to telling someone to 'Jump', and then being asked, 'How high?' Nevertheless, in a strange way it was a very bonding experience, a bit like a dysfunctional sisterhood, although at times the blows did fall below the belt.

One thing's for sure: you needed to be bullet-proof to survive the journey; that, and tough-skinned, with the ability to not care. But I did care. I was worried how the audience would receive the series. Would they slam me for wearing high heels on a tennis court or for speaking 'British' in the bathroom? I could only wait and see.

Once it became clear that the audience did support me as the series unfolded, I felt very relieved. The dynamics were such that initial friendships turned sour fairly quickly and I was left to fend for myself amongst a group of girls who had all turned nasty. The audience didn't like this. Some viewers threatened to turn off; they couldn't stand seeing me mistreated. Some of my friends cried watching it. Teresa couldn't watch at all, Bettina wasn't impressed by how I was treated, nor were my boys or my partner. But Mum was okay with it; she knew I could handle it.

When the cameras are rolling you forget they are there. It's difficult to maintain a façade for very long, and the truth is eventually revealed. I know this from my legal experience of in-house residential programs. The program is residential to allow for a client's true colours to be revealed. Behaviour can't be maintained if it's not really who they are; by the fourth day they are worn down and have dropped their guard. It was similar timing on the show. I went into the production thinking some of the women were my friends but within about four days, I knew the truth.

I became well known for my one-liners and for my ability to stay composed under pressure. Even when I was attacked by the others girls all at once, like an ambush, I was able to pull out my compact and powder my nose. There were also occasions when some of the girls, who were hell-bent on making their point, would harp on about the same thing, trying to get a rise out of me so they could validate their behaviour. But I refused to succumb and give them that satisfaction. Over the course of my career, I had seen a lot of abusive relationships and was well aware of the dynamic of the perpetrator: they are always looking to become the victim. They taunt and tease until they get a reaction and then point their finger and say, 'See, she deserved me treating her badly. This is who she really is.'

But I wasn't used to dealing with women who were emotionally charged. Through my work, I had only dealt with women who took pride in being level-headed. I had never been in a situation in which a group of women were looking to bring me down, plotting my demise. This behaviour was completely foreign to me. I had always been the one to jump in and defend someone who needed help; and although I wanted to at times, I wasn't about to put anyone in a rubbish bin and roll them down the stairs. I had come a long way since that incident.

Filming the show had been difficult but by the time it went to air, I had time to recover. Despite all the stress, the girls had given me a platform to entertain. They had inadvertently made it 'the Gina Liano show'. It became about me: what I said, what I was wearing, how much they disliked me, and it kept going for ten episodes. I was also described as being the most 'real' of the cast members. I was being myself and the audience could see this.

By the end of the series, my fans and followers were fiercely protective of me. They had become emotionally invested and they weren't going to put up with another bad word about me. If anyone suggested I had said or done something wrong, they would come back fighting. I didn't ever need to respond, someone else always had my back. I really appreciated all this encouragement and support; it sustained me. I hadn't realised the extent to which the audience would become involved in the show. In fact, some of the cast members were being abused and even attacked on the street. I wasn't very happy about this; all of us had stepped out of our comfort zones and it had taken a lot of courage to put ourselves in the public eye. After all, it was only entertainment, we were not saving lives.

As each week passed, my popularity soared. I was ranked the most popular housewife by seventy-four percent, with polls showing that ninety-three percent of viewers would not watch another season if I did not feature. I had become famous overnight.

My new challenge was to adapt to public recognition. It took me a while to realise that people knew who I was. I was still going to the supermarket and doing the usual things, but people approached me from every direction asking for a photo and an autograph. These days, everyone has a camera on their phone so as soon as one person stopped for a photo, a queue would form of more people hoping for the same opportunity.

I kept practising law throughout the show's season. I was trying to be discreet in court but even this became difficult. My clients were often surprised when I turned up to represent them, asking for a photo and calling their friends to tell them who their barrister was. And often even the opposing party would say, 'I know you, you're from that housewives show. I loved you on the show, can I have an autograph?'

Since the airing of the first season on Australian TV, the show has gone to the USA for broadcast on the same channel as the USA franchises. Despite being programmed into a difficult time-slot, it still rated very well, bringing a new wave of fans and followers. The show has since screened in the UK, with a similar reaction there.

I seriously tossed up whether I would participate in a second season. I had endured months of aggressive behaviour which had worn me down. I knew that the audience who had been sympathetic would lose compassion if I put myself back into the same situation. Only an idiot would do that.

I decided to come back for another season for a few reasons. The cast had changed so I knew the dynamic would be different. The first season had given me a platform to be entertaining, but I also knew that I had a lot more to give. I hoped that the new season would give me an opportunity to reveal a different aspect of my personality. Furthermore, I had drawn a large following and I didn't want to disappoint my fans by not reappearing. So I came back and gave it my best shot.

My family supported my decision to return, once again trusting that I could look after myself. They know I am a capable woman who can bring the wisdom of an incredible life's journey onto the show.

Since filming season one and two I have launched a shoe range. I'm also working on a costume jewellery range, have become an ambassador to the Cancer Council of Victoria and participated in many functions and charities. I've co-hosted television programs, featured as a guest on many shows and attended countless media interviews and photo shoots. I've attended the Logies and the Astras, and have been approached by various producers to participate in spin-off shows, both in Australia and the USA. I have also written my autobiography. All this in eighteen months.

Perhaps my adventurous life had been preparing me for this. Over the years, I'd learned to be open-minded and never surprised by the turns of fate. As a barrister, I'd seen and heard a lot. I was grateful for everything I'd experienced, although I never once imagined where it would all lead. I certainly hadn't anticipated that I'd be famous. Most people who reach celebrity status have been chasing it all their lives. I had only ever chased a law degree and a legal career. All the other chapters in my life were unplanned. Some were good, some were bad. Life just takes over and no-one knows their destiny. But sometimes you need to take a hold of what's in front of you, and you need to be fearless.

CHAPTER NINE

What I've Learned

I'VE LEARNED A lot over the years.

From my childhood, I learned how much I love my family and how much fun it can be for a child to be surrounded by chaos and festivities. Apparently, by the time you are six years old, you are the person you're going to be for the rest of your life. My mother and father had instilled many values in me by that age. I was taught to be honest and open and to have a sense of humour. My time at boarding school was my first negative life experience. It was only six months but it had a tremendous impact on my worldview. I grew up quickly and knew that I had to be strong. The experience also forged a strong bond between me and my sisters, which remains to this day.

From my mother I learned the fundamental principles on how to succeed in life. She taught me that with faith and wisdom, you can achieve your goal. I've learned that the role of a mother in a child's life is critical to their foundation as a person. My mother was, and still is, an exemplary role model. She continues to inspire me to be the woman I am today. Her love of fashion and her inner strength have always given me confidence to be who I am. She comes from a long line of strong women and I seem to have followed that lineage. I'm often asked how my mother managed to raise five successful children. As a mother, I've often pondered how she taught us about the world; that it was there for the taking. She taught us to be comfortable in our own skin, and to never be afraid of hard work. She insisted that everyone on this earth is equal and that we were no better than anyone. People are people and everyone is approachable. She balanced this with the realities of life and taught us to be wary and wise. She made sure we were never gullible or naive. She wanted us to have our eyes wide open.

Being a mother has been the best chapter of my life. I have enjoyed every day of it and look forward to becoming a grandmother one day. The truth is, I simply love life. I love the life in a person and I'm grateful for every day. I have watched my boys struggle with the prospect of losing me, which was very painful. The experience of cancer raised my level of compassion for anyone who has lost a parent.

My boys continue to teach me a lot about who I am, and I recognise the importance of my role in their life through my own experience with my mother. It was interesting to me that when I underwent cancer treatment and felt extremely vulnerable, the first person I wanted with me was my mother. It didn't matter that I was thirty-six. In my view, when push comes to shove there's no such thing as grown-ups. I had been strong without her from a young age and I continue to have a close, loving relationship with my mum.

I've learned that the human spirit is amazing and that love can conquer all. A lot can be said in few words. In fact, people quickly forget your words but they rarely forget how you made them feel. The universal language of love is not easily forgotten.

I've also learned that how a person behaves towards you is a reflection of them rather than of you. You can't be responsible for another person's behaviour; furthermore, you can only be responsible for what you say, not for what someone understands. It took me a long time to appreciate this concept. I always felt compelled to labour a point so that I was understood. My mother would often say, 'You can't breastfeed the world.' I have also learned that sometimes the less you care, the happier you will be. Some situations need to be left alone, and it's important to work out which situations fall into this category. The truth is I do care, but sometimes walking away is the best you can do.

I'm grateful for the people I have met along the way. They have taught me so much, whether the experiences were good or bad. From my teachers at school to the cast on *The Real Housewives of Melbourne*, I have learned when to walk away, when to let things go, and when to stay. I've learned to distinguish what is and isn't important.

I look forward to the years to come. So far I have had an interesting journey, and each experience has contributed to who I am today. Some chapters in my life have been challenging and I feel blessed to have survived them. I have lived courageously. My courage has been my resistance to fear. I have found courage through my faith and I have used fear as a motivator to step out and follow my dreams. I've managed to fly in the face of adversity and I've never been afraid to work hard to pursue my dreams. Right or wrong, you don't always have to be right as long as you're certain.

I decided at a young age to live my life my way, and with that I became fearless.